D0215992

DATE DUE

THE
COMPETITION
OF IDEAS

THE COMPETITION OF IDEAS

the world of the washington think tanks

MURRAY WEIDENBAUM

Transaction Publishers
New Brunswick (U.S.A.) and London (U.K.)

Library of Congress Catalog Number: 2008031102
ISBN: 978-1-4128-0833-0
Printed in the United States of America

Library of Congress Cataloging-in-Publication Data

Weidenbaum, Murray L.
    The competition of ideas : the world of Washington think tanks / Murray Weidenbaum.
        p. cm.
    Includes bibliographical references and index.
    ISBN 978-1-4128-0833-0 (acid-free paper)
    1. Government consultants--Washington Metropolitan Area. 2. Research institutes--Washington Metropolitan Area. 3. Policy scientists--Washington (D.C.) 4. United States--Politics and government--21st century. I. Title.

JK468.C7W45 2008
320.60973--dc22

                                                2008031102

Contents

Preface   vii

1. Introduction: The Challenge Facing Think Tanks   1

2. Basic Data on Washington Think Tanks   9

3. The Five Major Think Tanks (The "DC-5")   19

4. Making Some Comparisons   37

5. How Think Tanks Operate   49

6. Think Tanks and Business   67

7. Measuring the Influence of Think Tanks   87

8. Findings, Conclusions, and Recommendations   103

Index   117

Preface

This book was written during a sabbatical for research granted by Washington University. I am indebted to the University's Weidenbaum Center on the Economy, Government, and Public Policy for a great variety of support and to Steven Smith, the Center's director, for continued encouragement.

Helpful research assistance was provided by Pornsak Chandanab-humma, Jeremiah Pawlowicz, and Andrew Weidenbaum. As she has done on so many of my previous writings, Christine Moseley carefully typed and reviewed the various drafts of the manuscript with ever-present patience and good humor.

This analysis of the major Washington think tanks draws heavily on several decades of involvement in their activities. At different times I have been a visiting scholar at the American Enterprise Institute and the Center for Strategic and International Studies, as well as a speaker at meetings at the Brookings Institution, the Cato Institute, and the Heritage Foundation. I have also written for their publications, and served as a reviewer of ongoing studies.

However, I wrote this book from the vantage point of an independent college professor who sees the accomplishments as well as the shortcomings of these vital institutions. I hope that the findings, conclusions, and recommendations that I offer here will enhance the quality and effectiveness of their work.

Murray Weidenbaum

1

Introduction:
The Challenge Facing Think Tanks

Washington-based think tanks spend $411 million a year in a continuing battle for influence and attention in the world of national policymaking. Among them, five influential think tanks spend $140 million a year in a competition for attention in the dominant newspapers, on the nightly news, and in the halls of legislators. But a fundamental mismatch exists in the public policy community.

On reflection, the difficult and urgent problems facing the United States in the early 21st century require a more responsible and effective approach than vying for quotes in the media—or the *Congressional Record*. The strategically located think tank community can play a more useful role by rethinking the focus of its activities. This book is dedicated to encouraging these vital organizations to undertake the truly difficult tasks of reconciling competing interests and thus developing new approaches to public policy issues that are more likely to be adopted.

The Nature of the Challenge

The world of Washington, DC policymaking is a strange place for most Americans. Often that world is envisioned as a dark place, which is epitomized by bundles of money moving stealthily from wealthy special interests to powerful government decision makers. Yet, at other times, Washington, DC is the far more benign location for people who are expected to deal seriously with the pressing issues that face the nation—the threats of inflation and unemployment, getting and keeping health insurance, protecting the environment, and achieving a more peaceful world. The reality of the nation's capital is, of course, far more complex than either of these two oversimplified views.

The key people involved in making those vital decisions are not only the responsible federal officials and the folks who lobby them—and the

1

journalists who report their activity. What we can call the "Washington policy community" also includes a very special breed of organizations—neither in the government nor in the business community—known as "think tanks." Although they have been called "citadels for public intellectuals,"[1] those who work in those private, non-profit organizations do not just sit and think. They perform many important functions in the public policy process, even though they do not produce and sell goods and services, at least not in the conventional sense of those terms.

Think tanks are key sources of information and expertise for those who debate vital national issues in the halls of Congress as well as for the omnipresent media who report the ebbs and flows of power and influence in the nation's capital. Far more fundamentally, at times think tanks set the agenda for those important debates by focusing attention on emerging national concerns or presenting new approaches to solving problems already widely recognized. In total, although their impact is not widely appreciated beyond the Washington "beltway," think tanks play an active role in the complex process in which national public policy is made.

Nevertheless, think tanks are not omnipotent. Many of their tedious reports and ideological briefings are ignored, often deservedly so. Also, some think tank people—because of their lack of public policy experience or the pedestrian nature of their research—attract much less attention to their views than do other participants in national debates. On balance, however, examining that fascinating community of idea generators provides a key to understanding how public policy is made in the United States. That, in essence, is the task of this book.

The reader will learn that no think tank is quite as influential as it claims to be, especially in its messages to its financial supporters. Not every think tank researcher is brilliant or a person of great experience and judgment. Nor is every think tank report lucid or even relevant to the needs of the time. Far more often than not, there is a great deal of disagreement among think tanks and, at times, on the part of the staff members within an individual "tank." Not only is that independence of thought basic to this very special intellectual community. The resultant competition of ideas strengthens our free society. Over time, think tanks raise the level of debate in the nation and, warts and all, are a force for good.

However, my book is not a defense of the status quo. After identifying both the strengths and weaknesses of the major think tanks, I wind up with a host of findings and suggestions which are designed to change the way they operate—and also enhance the contribution that they make to public policy. At a time of wide and often bitter partisan divides on key issues, I try to show how, with substantial reorientation of their activities, think tanks can help the nation achieve some badly-needed higher common ground.

Despite the strategic role of think tanks, the public in general does not understand—and often is unaware of—the way they operate. Neither the business executives and individual citizens who support them nor the academics who look down their noses at them really know how think tanks function and influence governmental decision making. This study is written from the viewpoint of an analyst who has lived in the think tank world but who now tries to see this phenomenon from a more detached academic location.

Think tanks are known more formally as public policy research institutes. Most of them are free-standing private tax-exempt non-profit organizations whose support comes primarily from the private sector. The crucial output of think tanks is the illusive notion of impacting public policy decision making. Although thousands of organizations like to refer to themselves as think tanks, only a relatively few are broad-based and influential year in-year out in the public policy arena.

Not every organization with a research division is a think tank. An example of the confusion is a *New York Times* editorial favorably describing the Organization for Economic Cooperation and Development as "a governmental think tank."[2] On the contrary, the OECD is a large group of governments of industrialized nations. At its meetings, senior officials of those governments consider and pass resolutions on government policies (I used to be one of them). They are supported by a fine staff of economists and other analysts. However meritorious, the OECD is hardly a think tank of independent public policy "thinkers."

It is ironic that, although the activities of many think tanks enjoy extensive coverage in the nation's media, most professional analyses of think tanks as an institution yield very negative evaluations of their role. As we will see in the chapters that follow, the think tanks themselves provide and warrant a far more nuanced and often positive evaluation of their activities.

Citations from a variety of sources give the flavor of the negative concerns raised by the intellectual phenomenon known as think tanks:

> . . . the new think tanks have abandoned the tradition of detached scholarship.[3]

> The once civil and scholarly exchanges of ideas and information . . . have been transformed into a "war of ideas."[4]

The reign of the pensive, passive, pipe-smoking Washington think tank is under assault.[5]

The biggest worry . . . the trend for think tanks . . . to produce research that is little more than polemical commentary.[6]

. . . the serious dangers that privately-financed think tanks pose to a democratic society.[7]

. . . a think tank should be more than . . . the source of 15-second bites of expertise for the evening TV news.[8]

. . . a lot of tank, but not much think.[9]

To analyze these critical views, it is useful to understand that the basic strength of think tanks does not lie in their political or economic power. Rather, it is in the weight given by public policy decision makers to their expertise, the cogency of their arguments, the accuracy of their data, and the independence of their work. In a December 1988 speech, President Ronald Reagan referred to "the triumph of the think tank." He went on to state, ". . . today the most important American scholarship comes out of our think tanks."[10] Not all of Ronald Reagan's successors have shared his very positive and expansive attitude toward think tanks, yet these very special organizations have continued to flourish.

The stock in trade of think tanks is essentially a soft asset—information. Of course, think tank people do more than quietly research questions of public policy. In the words of one analyst, they "comment tirelessly on public issues."[11]

This study tries to enhance the understanding of think tanks while gauging their effectiveness. Thus my focus is on examining the interaction between the work of think tanks and the formation of public policy in the United States. At the outset, a brief description of the public policy process is useful. Researchers often use a four-stage model to highlight the process.

The Public Policy Process[12]

1. Development Stage

Public policy issues—be they environmental or economic or international—do not usually erupt full-blown. They evolve over time from persistent interactions and frictions between important sectors of society or from strong and continuing dissatisfaction on the part of a significant interest group or from a new challenge facing the nation. Many issues never get beyond this initial stage of concern but not action.

2. Politicization Stage

The trigger for generating national attention to an issue of public policy often comes from a dramatic event, such as a major disaster. The explosion of the Union Carbide chemical plant in Bhopal, India was followed by front-page coverage of environmental issues. The unexpected bankruptcy of Enron moved corporate governance from the university law reviews to the nightly news. The attack on the Twin Towers on September 11, 2001 generated an unprecedented interest in the hitherto boring subject of homeland security.

As a given problem commands more public attention, experts and advocates begin to comment. "Influentials"—academics, journalists, clergy, and think-tank analysts—participate actively in this phase of the public policy process. Activist organizations adopt the issue. The issue itself may acquire an attractive label: fair housing, clean air, immigration reform, etc. In many cases, the issue ultimately makes its way into the mass media, where it is popularized.

3. Legislative Stage

As issues generate widespread interest, pressures develop to resolve the problems involved. Often—but not inevitably—these pressures result in legislative hearings followed by the passage of new laws. The Sarbanes-Oxley corporate governance reforms were enacted less than two years after the highly-publicized Enron bankruptcy.

Thus, it may take many months or even several years for an issue to result in passage of specific legislation. The first significant bill to regulate employee pensions was introduced in 1967 and the Employee Retirement Income Security Act was passed seven years later, in 1974. Frequently, the pressing issue of today melts away before changes are made in public policy. In that manner, the notion of a national planning system for the United States, popular in the 1970s, never got beyond the politicization stage.

On the other hand, when the Secretary of the Treasury in 1969 issued a list of wealthy people who did not pay any federal income tax, Congress quickly responded by passing a new Alternative Minimum Tax, which is still with us.

4. Implementation Stage

The final phase of the public policy process begins after the enabling legislation has been passed. The designated government organization starts to write and then issue the rules and procedures needed to carry out the law. Each year, federal departments and agencies issue thousands of pages of such new regulations. That is when compliance by the private sector begins. Interest groups, including public interest law firms, often challenge the execution of the law. In the process, they may delay the time at which the new law takes effect or the manner in which it is carried out.

There is nothing inevitable in the process just described, nor does each successful issue go through the four-step public policy process in the neat demarcations implied here. Most relevant to this study, rarely—if ever—does a given think tank participate in, and much less influence, the actions taken in each of the four stages of the development of a given issue.

Experienced participants in the public policy process report that there are many different players in each stage of the process. These players include idea people, special interests and those who lobby for them, media and other "middlemen," members of Congress including leaders and their staffs, executive branch policymakers and career analysts, and on occasion the members of the judiciary who may endorse or reject specific policy actions taken by the other two branches of government.

On occasion, think tanks are heavily involved in generating ideas in phase one; tax reform is a good example. Most of the time, however, think tanks devote their major resources to the second stage of the public policy process, where opinion on an issue of public policy is mobilized. Developing and publicizing specific proposals for reforming government regulation of business are a good continuing example. At times, a think tank's work may be influential in the early development stage, while quite a few find their staff members heavily involved in preparing specific provisions of proposed new laws. On occasion, think tank staff members may join together in presenting an "amicus curiae" brief urging a course of action on a court considering an important issue of public policy.

No standard pattern emerges from my examination of recent experience. Individual researchers and analysts at think tanks come with a variety of professional backgrounds and participate in the public policy process in many different ways, especially as they interact with the other players. There surely is no ivory tower where think tank researchers can hide from the daily pressures of the public policy process.

Issues to Grapple With

The motivation for writing this book goes beyond the important task of improving the public's understanding of how Washington think tanks operate. After developing the necessary foundation of knowledge about the strengths and weaknesses of these very special organizations, we will have the opportunity to try to enhance their contribution to the formation of public policy in the United States.

Thus, this study raises and then attempts to answer a variety of questions about think tanks:

- What do they really do?
- Are think tanks truly independent analysts of ideas and issues?
- Can a line be drawn between activism and scholarship? Should such a line be drawn?
- Are think tanks important players in the public policy process?
- How can think tanks improve the quality of their work?
- What limits should think tanks place on the range of their activities?
- Looking at think tanks and universities, how alike are they? How different are they?
- Is competition among think tanks always desirable? Would their overall effectiveness be increased if at times they searched for common ground?

As we will see in the chapters that follow, answering these questions often leads to raising additional questions. In large part, that iterative process reflects the complicated nature of think tanks and the variety of relationships within the think tank community as well as its many interactions with the rest of society. Given the caliber of their resources and their special relationships with governmental decision makers, think tanks have a unique potential to make important new contributions to public policy in the years ahead.

* * *

Please note: Chapter 2 presents a new database for analyzing Washington-based think tanks. Those readers who have a low tolerance for statistics can move directly to Chapter 3.

Notes

1. Robert J. Samuelson, "Making the Think Tank Think," *Washington Post*, August 1, 2007, p. A17.
2. "The Land of Opportunity?" *New York Times*, July 13, 2007, p. A20.
3. Louis Jacobson, "Tanks on the Roll," *National Journal*, July 8, 1995, p. 1767.
4. James McGann, *Responding to 9/11: Are Think Tanks Thinking Outside the Box?* (Philadelphia: Foreign Policy Research Institute, 2003), p. 54.
5. Amy Wilentz, "On the Intellectual Ramparts," *Time*, September 1, 1986, p. 22.
6. Andrew Rich, *Think Tanks, Public Policy, and the Politics of Expertise* (Cambridge: Cambridge University Press, 2004), p. 220.
7. Sandi E. Cooper, "Why Big Guns in War of Ideas Line Up on Right," *New York Times*, August 21, 1994, p. 14E.
8. William Safire, "Tanks for the Memory," *New York Times*, September 1, 1986, p. A23.
9. Guy de Jonquieres, "Asia Needs a More Active Market in Ideas," *Financial Times*, August 31, 2006, p. 17.
10. Cited in American Enterprise Institute, *1988-1989 Annual Report*, p. 3.
11. James Allen Smith, *The Idea Brokers: Think Tanks and the Rise of the New Policy Elite* (New York: Free Press, 1991), p. xiii.
12. Adapted from Murray L. Weidenbaum, *Business and Government in the Global Marketplace*, Seventh Edition (Upper Saddle River, NJ: Pearson Prentice-Hall, 2004), pp. 314-318.

2

Basic Data on Washington Think Tanks

This chapter develops a database that covers thirty-two independent and private think tanks that are operating in the Washington, DC metropolitan area. These thirty-two cover a wide array of research and policy analysis, ranging from the prominent and broad-based activities of the Brookings Institution and the American Enterprise Institute to the very small and specialized organizations such as the Institute for Research on the Economics of Taxation. The specific number (thirty-two) excludes many organizations that have some of the attributes of a public policy research organization, but which are affiliated with universities, governments, or private interest groups. Thus, this chapter deals with Washington area think tanks that are both private and independent.

The data in this chapter were obtained from a public record, the special tax returns submitted by think tanks and other non-profit institutions, IRS Form 990, "Return of Organization Exempt from Income Tax." The Form 990 data are not always identical to the numbers contained in annual reports or similar materials provided by these organizations but the differences are not substantial.

In the aggregate, the thirty-two think tanks reported that they spent $411.3 million in 2005. For purposes of analysis, it is useful to divide these think tanks into three admittedly arbitrary categories: (1) large and diversified, (2) large and specialized, and (3) small and specialized (see Table 2.1).

Subsequent chapters will focus on five Washington-based think tanks which are here labeled "large and diversified." They are the American Enterprise Institute (AEI), the Brookings Institution, the Center for Strategic and International Studies (CSIS), the Cato Institute, and the Heritage Foundation. They often will be referred to as the DC-5. Unlike the twenty-seven others, these five are highly visible in the public

Table 2.1
Expenditures of DC-Based Think Tanks in 2005

Category and Organization	Amount (in millions)
Large and Diversified	
Brookings Institution	$38.4
Heritage Foundation	35.5
Center for Strategic and International Studies	27.2
American Enterprise Institute	21.4
Cato Institute	17.1
Subtotal	$139.6
Large and Specialized	
Urban Institute	$74.2
Aspen Institute	54.9
Carnegie Endowment for International Peace	20.6
World Resources Institute	20.1
Center for American Progress	16.2
Center on Budget & Policy Priorities	12.8
Resources for the Future	10.2
Subtotal	$209.0
Small and Specialized	
Peterson Institute for International Economics	$8.0
New America Foundation	6.3
Economic Policy Institute	5.4
Joint Center for Political & Economic Studies	5.4
World Security Institute	5.4
Committee for Economic Development	4.0
Competitive Enterprise Institute	3.1
Institute for Policy Studies	2.9
Worldwatch Institute	2.8
Progress & Freedom Foundation	2.7*
Atlantic Council	2.5
Progressive Policy Institute**	2.5
Lexington Institute	2.2
Overseas Development Council	2.2#
Center for the Study of the Presidency	1.8
Ethics & Public Policy Center	1.7
Tax Foundation	1.7
Economic Strategy Institute	0.8
Earth Policy Institute	0.7
Institute for Research on the Economics of Taxation	0.6
Subtotal	$62.7
Grand Total	$411.3

* Data for 2004.
# Data for 2000.
** Data for Third Way Foundation, which finances the Institute.
Source: IRS Forms 990, "Return of Organization Exempt From Income Tax," 2005.

policy arena and their research and publications cover a wide assortment of domestic and international issues (Chapter 3 presents details of their activities).

The seven think tanks here listed as "large and specialized" tend to focus their efforts on important but specific aspects of public policy. The largest of them, the Urban Institute, receives the bulk of its funding from government agencies and its researchers are not as involved in the daily public policy battles as the DC-5. Nevertheless, on some important domestic issues, notably tax policy, the views of Urban Institute specialists are frequently elicited by journalists and legislators.

The Aspen Institute has moved its headquarters to the Washington area quite recently but so far has concentrated on longer-term aspects of national policy. In contrast, the Carnegie Endowment for International Peace has a long-term presence in the nation's capital, but limits its role to foreign policy. Resources for the Future and the Peterson Institute for International Economics are cogent examples of specialized and highly regarded think tanks.

Some of the smaller think tanks on occasion can be quite influential in the specific areas in which they specialize. For example, because the Institute for Policy Studies is the most conspicuous DC-based think tank on the far left of the political spectrum, at times the national media afford its reports and representatives very substantial coverage. This reflects their attempts to provide balance and variety in reporting on controversies in public policy.

Not all of the thirty-two Washington-based think tanks directly compete against each other for influence or money. Nonetheless, it is illuminating to develop some measures of this special sector of the economy, which are similar to those used in analyzing the degrees of concentration and competition in the business marketplace.

A relatively small number of organizations dominate the Washington-based think tank sector (see Table 2.2). For example, the DC-5 represents one third of the annual outlays of the thirty-two think tanks and the ten largest account for about four fifths of the total.

Some Interesting Detail

The available data also contain other insights into the status of the Washington-based think tanks. For example, for most of them, their current financial health appears to be sound; twenty out of thirty-two report a surplus of revenues over expenditures. As shown in Table 2.3, a few of those surpluses in 2005 are quite substantial—$21 million in the case of the Carnegie Endowment for International Peace and $11 million for the Heritage Foundation. Some of the relatively large excesses of revenues over current expenditures, however, reflect the results of episodic fund-raising drives. On the other hand, twelve of the smaller think tanks keep a close balance between income and outgo, with surpluses or deficits of $200,000 or less.

Another way of assessing the relative power of think tanks is to examine their continuing financial strength as measured by their net assets or fund balances (see Table 2.4). Such numbers provide an important indicator of the ability of the organization to weather a difficult period of substantial reduction in new funding. Endowment funds also generate current income, which becomes available without additional fundraising effort. As shown in Table 2.2, these fund balances are more concentrated in a relatively few think tanks than are measures of annual outlays. The DC-5 holds 45 percent of the net assets of the thirty-two tanks in my database and the top 10 hold nine-tenths of the total balances.

With a few exceptions (eight out of thirty-two), the Washington-based think tanks rely entirely on private financing, with varying dependence on foundations, corporations, and private companies. Only two—the Urban Institute and the World Resources Institute—receive grant support from the government in excess of $1 million a year (see Table 2.5).[1] The Urban Institute is unusual in that the total of government grants exceeds private sector support ($49 million out of a total of $85 million in 2005).

Table 2.2
Measures of Concentration and Competition Among
DC-Based Think Tanks in 2005

Think Tank Category	Expenditures	Net Assets
	(percentages of totals)	
DC-5	34%	45%
Top 10	79	89
Top 20	95	99
Bottom 12	5	1

Source: Computed from Tables 2.1 and 2.4.

Table 2.3
Surplus or Deficits of DC-Based Think Tanks in 2005
(in millions)

Organization	Surplus or Deficit
American Enterprise Institute	$12.3
Aspen Institute	13.6
Atlantic Council	(0.2)
Brookings Institution	9.9
Carnegie Endowment for International Peace	21.3
Cato Institute	5.6
Center for American Progress	7.1
Center for Strategic & International Studies	2.9
Center for the Study of the Presidency	(*)
Committee for Economic Development	1.0
Center on Budget & Policy Priorities	2.5
Competitive Enterprise Institute	0.1
Earth Policy Institute	(0.1)
Economic Policy Institute	0.1
Economic Strategy Institute	(0.2)
Ethics & Public Policy Center	0.2
Heritage Foundation	10.9
Institute for Policy Studies	0.2
Institute for Research on the Economics of Taxation	*
Joint Center for Political & Economic Studies	(0.6)
Lexington Institute	0.1
New America Foundation	2.8
Overseas Development Council	(1.3)
Peterson Institute for International Economics	(0.5)
Progress & Freedom Foundation	0.5
Progressive Policy Institute (Third Way Foundation)	(0.4)
Resources for the Future	17.6
Tax Foundation	0.2
Urban Institute	5.6
World Resources Institute	(1.5)
World Security Institute	(1.9)
Worldwatch Institute	(0.3)

* = Less than $50,000.
Note: Numbers in parentheses indicate negative values.

Source: IRS Forms 990, "Return of Organization Exempt From Income Tax," 2005.

Table 2.4
Net Assets or Fund Balances of DC-Based Think Tanks
At Year End 2005

Organization	Amount (in millions)
Brookings Institution	$269.7
Carnegie Endowment for International Peace	202.7
Heritage Foundation	137.3
Aspen Institute	108.0
Urban Institute	93.4
American Enterprise Institute	69.3
Resources for the Future	49.0
World Resources Institute	46.5
Center for Strategic & International Studies	34.4
Center on Budget & Policy Priorities	30.9
Peterson Institute for International Economics	30.6
Center for American Progress	21.9
Cato Institute	21.5
World Security Institute	12.2
Joint Center for Political & Economic Studies	9.1
New America Foundation	6.4
Committee for Economic Development	4.4
Atlantic Council	3.8
Economic Policy Institute	3.7
Lexington Institute	3.1
Center for the Study of the Presidency	2.3
Competitive Enterprise Institute	1.8
Ethics & Public Policy Center	1.4
Institute for Policy Studies	1.3
Earth Policy Institute	1.0
Progress & Freedom Foundation	0.9
Progressive Policy Institute (Third Way Foundation)	0.9
Tax Foundation	0.9
Worldwatch Institute	0.8
Economic Strategy Institute	0.4
Institute for Research on the Economics of Taxation	0.1
Overseas Development Council	*
Total	$1,169.7

* = Less than $100.000.
Source: IRS Forms 990, "Return of Organization Exempt From Income Tax," 2005.

Table 2.5
Government Grants to DC-Based Think Tanks in 2005

Organization	Amount
Aspen Institute	$58,334
Atlantic Council	464,986
Brookings Institution	775,586
Center for Strategic & International Studies	57,095
Resources for the Future	2,124,480
Urban Institute	49,457,281
World Resources Institute	3,954,631
Worldwatch Institute	515,620

Source: IRS Forms 990, "Return of Organization Exempt From Income Tax," 2005.

Among the great detail required by IRS Form 990 is a report on lobbying expense. Only five of the thirty-two DC-based think tanks report any expenditures for lobbying: the Center for American Progress, the Committee for Economic Development, the Center on Budget and Policy Priorities, the Competitive Enterprise Institute, and the New American Foundation. The largest amount of lobbying expense was incurred by the Center on Budget and Policy Priorities, approximately $600,000 or less than 7 percent of its annual expenditures. Thus, direct lobbying is clearly not a significant activity on the part of the DC-based think tanks.

The Form 990 also contains information on the compensation of the leaders of the reporting non-profit institutions. Table 2.6 shows the annual compensation for the CEOs of Washington-based think tanks. The formal data literally range from over $600,000 to zero. In the absence of quantitative measures of effectiveness, it is difficult to relate the compensation practices of a given think tank to those of its peers.

Yet, even a cursory examination of the data in this chapter reveals a positive relationship between CEO compensation and size of the organization, especially measured by its expenditures. In research on the corporate sector some years ago, I found a similar positive relationship between CEO compensation and the size of the firm measured by sales.[2] Aside from concerns about motivation and incentive, there does seem to be some justification for paying somebody more to run a large enterprise than a smaller one in the same sector of the economy.

Table 2.6
Annual Compensation of Think Tank CEOs in 2005

Organization	Amount
$500,000 and over	
Heritage Foundation	$634,000
American Enterprise Institute	600,000
$250,000-$500,000	
Aspen Institute	450,000
Cato Institute	408,000
CSIS	373,000
Carnegie Endowment	365,000
Urban Institute	341,000
Lexington Institute	325,000
Brookings Institution	309,000
Joint Center for Political & Economic Studies	300,000
Committee for Economic Development	282,000
World Resources Institute	282,000
World Security Institute	258,000
$100,000-$250,000	
Progress and Freedom Foundation	235,000
Center for American Progress	234,000
Peterson Institute for International Economics	204,000
Economic Policy Institute	201,000
Resources for the Future	200,000
Competitive Enterprise Institute	186,000
New American Foundation	178,000
Economic Strategy Institute	169,000
Progressive Policy Institute (Third Way Foundation)	167,000
Center on Budget & Policy Priorities	160,000
Overseas Development Council	152,000[+]
Ethics & Public Policy Center	148,000
Center for the Study of the Presidency	139,000
Tax Foundation	125,000
Less than $100,000	
Worldwatch Institute	95,000
Institute for Policy Studies	85,000
Institute for Research on the Economics of Taxation	85,000
Atlantic Council[o]	0
Earth Policy Institute	0

[+] Data for 2000.
[o] Acting president serving without pay.
Note: Data rounded to nearest $1,000.

Source: IRS Forms 990, "Return of Organization Exempt From Income Tax," 2005.

Conclusions

The DC-5 represents a very substantial portion of the activity (about one third) of the thirty-two Washington-based think tanks covered in this chapter. As a testament to their long-term sustainability, however, the DC-5 holds a more substantial share of the group's net assets—45 percent. Also, the challenges facing the leadership of the DC-5 are reflected in the above-average compensation of their leaders.

The rest of this book focuses on five major Washington-based think tanks, the DC-5. Doing so has enabled me to delve into specific issues about the important role of public policy research institutes in the nation's capital in a way that would not have been feasible if I had to examine the role of all the thirty-two think tanks operating in the national capital.

Notes

1. The IRS reports generally show the amount of government grants received by a think tank, often omitting contracts awarded by federal agencies.
2. Murray Weidenbaum, "Takeovers and Stockholders: Winners and Losers," *California Management Review*, Summer 1987.

3

The Five Major Think Tanks (The "DC-5")

This study tries to illuminate some of the unappreciated ways that public policy is developed in the United States. It does so by focusing on five major Washington-based private nonprofit organizations commonly referred to as "think tanks." They were selected because they are much broader based than the other think tanks that operate in the nation's capital. The work of these five covers both domestic and international issues, including military and civilian aspects, as well as economic, social, and political matters. The five are the American Enterprise Institute for Public Policy Research (AEI), the Brookings Institution (Brookings), the Cato Institute (Cato), the Center for Strategic and International Studies (CSIS), and the Heritage Foundation (Heritage). As a group, they will be referred to occasionally in the pages that follow as the DC-5.

The focus on policy research organizations located in the Washington area mirrors the earlier move of trade associations and other interest groups to the national capital. This geographic concentration reflects the continued importance of the federal government in the nation's decision making. The "tilt toward Washington, DC as the center of influence" has been noted in earlier studies of public policy think tanks.[1]

Each of these five has a relatively long-term presence in the nation's capital and has demonstrated the ability to devote substantial amounts of professional resources to a variety of important issues of national policy. Typically, their major efforts, as well as many minor ones, receive the attention of the national media as well as decision makers in both the public and private sectors.

The purpose of this chapter is to present pertinent basic information about each of the DC-5. The following chapter develops some generalizations from their combined experiences. No particular effort is made to evaluate the performance of any of the five organizations. A personal note:

in different ways, I have been involved with each of the DC-5 and I believe that has given me special insight into these specific think tanks.

The material that follows avoids repeating the detailed and interesting history of these organizations or of think tanks in general. Several scholars already have done so in a very systematic and comprehensive manner.[2] This study is more concerned with the current and, especially, the future role of these very distinctive organizations. Thus, except to illustrate a specific point, little reference will be made to the activities of think tanks in earlier time periods beyond the recent past.

The Brookings Institution

Brookings is the grandfather of Washington-based think tanks and is the largest of the DC-5 (see Chapter 4 for details). It grew out of the progressive era belief that public policy should be informed by disinterested expertise and social science research. However, individual staff members do not hesitate to take controversial positions on specific public policy issues, but the organization itself does not do so.

Brookings describes itself in rather general terms as "a private non-profit organization devoted to independent research and innovative policy solutions"[3] (see Table 3-1). According to its official statements, Brookings performs its research to "inform the public debate" rather than to advance a political agenda. Alice Rivlin, a long-term staff member who also has served in senior positions in government, describes Brookings as "a collection of scholars whose allegiance is to their discipline."[4]

Although it avoids a simple "party line," it is more likely that any one of those scholars has served in a Democratic rather than a Republican administration.

The organization devotes a substantial amount of its funds to formal educational activities. Its Center for Executive Education spent $4.7 million in 2005 (16 percent of Brookings' total program expenses) in providing continuing education on foreign and domestic policy issues for corporate and federal executives. The organization also conducts a program of policy education for members of the judiciary, financed with substantial business support. As is the case for the other major Washington-based think tanks, Brookings assigns considerable resources to attracting media coverage. It has built its own TV studio to give its scholars ready access to the airwaves.[5]

Brookings obtains its financing from a wide variety of foundations, companies, and individuals. One critical analyst reports that Brookings has produced more than "value-free" research. He refers to the numer-

Table 3.1
Highlights of the Brookings Institution

Headquarters
1775 Massachusetts Avenue NW
Washington, DC 20036

Date Founded: 1927 (predecessor organization established in 1916)

Official Purpose

To bring knowledge to bear on the current and emerging public policy problems facing the American people

Main Areas of Focus

Foreign Policy
Economic Studies
Metropolitan Policy
Government Studies
Global Economy and Development

Size of Staff

More than 140 resident and non-resident scholars; over 200 research assistants and support staff

Leadership

CEO: Strobe Talbott

Some Key Research Staff

James Steinberg, Foreign Policy
Thomas Mann, Political Science
William Gale, Economics
Martin Indyk, Foreign Policy

Governance

44 member Board of Trustees

Revenues and Expenses, Fiscal Year 2005
Operating revenues: $47.8 million
Operating expenses: $41.2 million
(Fundraising: $2.2 million)

Source: Brookings Institution (annual reports and other documents).

ous connections of Brookings staff in the network that comprises the long-term Washington establishment.[6] Indeed, some senior staff as well as several members of the board of trustees are considered to be "old Washington hands," having served in a variety of full-time and part-time governmental positions. Nevertheless, Strobe Talbott, Brookings' president, states that the organization strives to "bridge the partisan divide," especially in its joint efforts with other organizations. Yet, he cautions, to be nonpartisan does not mean to be policy-neutral.[7]

The major output of the organization is in the form of books on public policy issues written by its resident senior staff and some outside or "adjunct" scholars. Brookings conducts a limited amount of unclassified studies under government contract, reserving the right to publish the results on its own. Many of the staff members of Brookings have come from major university faculties (some of them are at Brookings on a part-time or temporary basis). Its roster of senior researchers includes several former presidents of major professional societies and others who are highly regarded by their professional colleagues. In academic and foundation circles, the organization is usually considered to be in "the mainstream." Many business and conservative leaders, in contrast, consider Brookings to be "liberal." The highly regarded Washington journalist Robert Samuelson recently identified a group of DC-based think tanks as either "liberal" or "conservative." He readily placed Brookings in the liberal category.[8]

Brookings has a well-established practice of quality control via a formal peer review process for its books and working papers, which reaches out to experts beyond its own staff (on occasion, I have been one of those outside reviewers). Brookings scholars believe that the key way of maintaining the quality of its research is less formal: the published research "must pass muster among our academic colleagues in the profession."[9]

Judging by the frequency of their appearances on the programs of professional society meetings and the positive reviews of Brookings publications in the learned journals, as a general proposition, the organization does "pass muster." Brookings also emphasizes the need to set up walls between funders and scholars. The importance of its large endowment is emphasized in this connection.[10]

The newest program initiated at Brookings is the Hamilton Project, launched in 2006 with the stated purpose of developing and advancing new policy ideas aimed at a stronger economy. The official project materials are couched in non-partisan language and one of its major reports on reforming health care was prepared by a senior researcher at the Heritage Foundation.[11] However, the *New York Times* reports that the Hamilton Project was initiated ". . . mostly by moderate Democrats from business and academia. . ."[12] An inspection of the list of the Project's personnel and advisers confirms that. Brookings' response is that the Hamilton Project is best seen as a "boutique department" in a large department store.[13]

Brookings engages cooperatively with other think tanks and nonprofit institutions on subjects of joint interest (the most durable joint venture is with the American Enterprise Institute, as described a little later). One of the most visible joint activities was the Fiscal Wakeup Tour, which, in 2006, hosted events across the country to publicize long-term U.S. budget problems. Experts from a variety of other organizations participated, including the Concord Coalition, the Heritage Foundation, and the Government Accountability Office. Brookings' government studies program also has conducted research activities in collaboration with the Hoover Institution at Stanford University.[14]

The American Enterprise Institute

Developed in part as a conservative alternative to Brookings, the American Enterprise Institute for Public Policy Research (AEI) is the second oldest of the five DC-based think tanks (see Table 3-2). The late William Baroody, Sr., who is universally credited with building the organization, adopted the motto, "Competition of ideas is fundamental to a free society." AEI researchers at times disagree among themselves on specific policy issues. The Institute maintains that no attempt is made to develop a consensus or an institutional position. However, in the traditional liberal-conservative dichotomy in the policy arena, AEI is invariably listed as conservative.[15]

AEI's stated purposes are not value-free: "to defend the principles and improve the institutions of American freedom and democratic capitalism. . . ."[16] It claims to operate at "the intersection of scholarship and politics." Its scholars cover a very wide array of economic, national security, political, and social issues and write books, reports, and shorter articles for newspapers and magazines. More than 100 policy experts at a variety of American universities serve as adjunct scholars who prepare papers, studies, and monographs (for many years, I was one of those policy experts). Because of the broad range of program activities, AEI has been called "the MGM of Washington think tanks."[17]

AEI states that its president is responsible for setting its research agenda. The substance and conclusions of its research are determined

Table 3.2
Highlights of American Enterprise Institute

Headquarters
1150 17th Street NW
Washington, DC 20006

Date Founded: 1943

Official Purpose

Educational research

Main Areas of Focus

Economics
Defense and Foreign Policy
Social and Political Studies

Size of Staff

Approximately 175 at AEI Headquarters, 50-60 interns, and about 100 adjunct scholars

Leadership

CEO: Christopher DeMuth

Some Key Research Staff

Douglas Besharov, Social Studies
Michael Greve, Legal Studies
Kevin Hassett, Economic Policy
Charles Murray, Social Studies

Governance

25 member Board of Trustees

Revenues and Expenses, 2005

Revenue: $37.9 million
Expenses: $21.4 million
   (Fundraising: $8.6 million)

Source: American Enterprise Institute for Public Policy Research (annual reports and other documents).

by those who conduct the research. Many of the senior researchers came from academia and quite a few from Republican administrations or they leave to accept positions with Republican presidents.

The year 2006 provided several examples of the flow of people between a think tank such as AEI and the federal government. The editor of AEI's flagship magazine, Karl Zinsmeister, was appointed by President George W. Bush to be domestic policy chief in the White House. Visiting scholar Randall Krozner was appointed to the Board of Governors of the Federal Reserve System and resident scholar Phillip Swagel left to become Assistant Secretary of the Treasury for Economic Policy.

Moving in the other direction, Mark McClellan, formerly administrator of Medicaid and Medicare (and earlier a member of President Bush's Council of Economic Advisers), joined the AEI-Brookings Joint Center for Regulatory Studies. Also, Scott Gottlieb, former deputy commissioner of the Food and Drug Administration, returned to AEI. (As a matter of policy, AEI does not take any grants from government agencies.)

Almost bordering on "man bites dog," Brookings and AEI have joined forces in sponsoring a substantial and well-regarded program of research and analysis in the field of government regulation. The scholars at the Joint Regulatory Center have written a variety of books, reports, and articles on various aspects of regulation; at times they have been called upon to testify before congressional committees. Seeing the success of this innovative undertaking, Brookings subsequently established a program on tax policy conducted jointly with the Urban Institute. In a more limited venture, AEI and the Pacific Research Institute jointly publish an annual *Index of Leading Environmental Indicators.*

AEI President Christopher DeMuth states that the organization attempts to maintain quality control of its research primarily by hiring outstanding people. It usually asks two to three outside experts to review a manuscript prior to publication, with one of the reviewers "in fundamental disagreement with the author's approach." For some studies, a workshop of about fifteen people meets to discuss the manuscript, each participant being expected to read the work in advance of the meeting. The large majority of the workshop participants are academics and practitioners (from business, government, and journalism), rather than AEI staff members.

AEI also has a long-standing eleven-member Council of Academic Advisers who review the research agenda, publications, and staff appointments. Council members are well-known faculty at major universities and I am one of them.

As in the case of Brookings, independence from financial supporters is achieved by having a wide diversity of revenue sources. DeMuth contends that very few attempts are ever made to influence a specific report. However, AEI's free-market orientation in its research on trade policy and telecommunications resulted in losing some business support.[18]

The Center for Strategic and International Studies

Founded as the Center for Strategic Studies, an autonomous part of Georgetown University, CSIS became an independent organization in 1986 (see Table 3-3). The Center, in its own words, "seeks to advance global security and prosperity in an era of economic and political transformation by providing strategic insights and practical policy solutions to decision makers."[19] The output of CSIS consists in part of monographs, reports, and other shorter contributions to newspapers and magazines. However, CSIS President John Hamre stresses the vital importance of oral briefings to policy makers to assist them in their decision making. "We want to change policy, not just write books."[20]

The original focus of CSIS was on foreign and military policy, and that continues to be its area of primary activity. However, it also has covered important domestic issues, ranging from environmental and energy questions to demographic trends to economic and fiscal policy. For example, a 1992 study suggested establishing a National Economic Council; the Clinton Administration followed this advice.[21] CSIS senior staff members include many former government officials (Republican and Democratic as well as some who consider themselves to be non-political) plus those who came from universities and other non-profit sectors.

CSIS is usually described as a middle-of-the-road organization. In a 2005 survey, *International Economy* magazine reported that CSIS was one of only two think tanks that were considered by Congress and the media as being neutral and nonpartisan (the other think tank was the Peterson Institute for International Economics).[22] On occasion, CSIS has joined forces with other, more specialized think tanks. For example, in 2006, it was one of four sponsoring organizations of the bipartisan Iraq Study Group (ISG) co-chaired by former Secretary of State James A. Baker and former member of the House of Representatives Lee Hamilton. Together with the U.S. Institute of Peace, the Baker Institute of Rice University, and the Center for the Study of the Presidency, CSIS provided support staff for the ISG.

In November 2006, CSIS and the Stanley Foundation of Muscatine, Iowa co-sponsored a two-day conference, "Building an Open and In-

Table 3.3
Highlights of Center for Strategic and International Studies

Headquarters
1800 K Street NW
Washington, DC 20006

Date Founded: 1962 (originally Center for Strategic Studies at Georgetown University)

Official Purpose

To inform and shape selected policy decisions in government and the private sector to meet the increasingly complex and difficult challenges that leaders will confront in the next century

Main Areas of Focus

Defense Policy and International Security
New Drivers of Global Security
Regional Programs

Size of Staff

Full-time: 220 plus affiliated experts

Leadership

CEO: John Hamre

Some Key Research Staff

Robert Einhorn, Defense Studies
Michele Flournoy, Defense Studies
Steve Morrison, African Studies
Erik Peterson, Strategic Studies

Governance
32 member Board of Trustees

Revenues and Expenses in 2005

Operating revenue:	$27.2 million
Expenditures:	$27.1 million
(Development:	$1.1 million)

Source: Center for Strategic and International Studies (annual reports and other documents).

clusive Regional Architecture for Asia." Participants included scholars from Asian universities and think tanks, as well as representatives of Brookings, RAND, and the Stanford Law School.[23]

Rather than sharpening the lines of debate or providing intellectual ammunition for one side of that debate, CSIS usually favors an informal and consensual approach to policymaking. Senators and representatives and other officials from both parties are actively involved in many CSIS-sponsored committees and commissions that study major program areas and attempt to develop new policies in a bipartisan fashion. For example, the CSIS-sponsored Commission on Public Infrastructure is co-chaired by former Republican senator Warren Rudman and former Clinton administration ambassador Felix Rohatyn.

James Allen Smith, a highly regarded analyst of think tanks, states that the "scholar-statesmen" of CSIS have tended to operate within a loose institutional framework in which talk and informal debates are more important than scholarly research and publication.[24] On the other hand, Zbigniew Brzezinski, the former national security adviser to President Jimmy Carter and a long-time member of the CSIS senior staff, has written very respectfully of the organization's "creative blend of strategy, diplomacy, and economics, as well as its unique mix of scholarship and practical involvement in key policy issues."[25]

CSIS, like the other major think tanks, supplements its full-time staff with a large network of affiliated, part-time experts. The directory of scholars at CSIS has been described as reading like a "who's who in Washington's foreign policymaking community."[26] Indeed, many distinguished former military and foreign policy officials have maintained an affiliation with CSIS as "counselors." Current examples include three former secretaries of defense (Harold Brown, Frank Carlucci, and James Schlesinger), two former national security advisers (Zbigniew Brzezinski and Brent Scowcroft), two former trade representatives (William Brock and Carla Hills), and one former chair of the Senate Armed Services Committee (Sam Nunn).

CSIS states that it maintains quality most fundamentally by trying to hire good people and not retaining those who are disappointing in their performance. Like the other think tanks there is no permanent guarantee of "tenure," so common at American colleges and universities. A formal quality review process, including outside reviewers, operates for the books and reports published by the CSIS Press and for the articles in its journal, *The Washington Quarterly*. CSIS also considers very seriously feedback from the users of its analysis, particularly those who support the research.

Heritage Foundation

The Heritage Foundation is frequently described as the prototypical advocacy think tank (see Table 3-4). Heritage from the outset has positioned itself as an active participant in public policy issues: "We draw solutions to contemporary problems from the ideas, principles, and traditions that make America great."[27] More specifically, the organization states that it strives to be "a leadership institution" that is instrumental in building "a more effective conservative movement." The main focus of its publications and activities is the U.S. Congress. However, Heritage maintained an especially active set of relationships with the Reagan administration.

Heritage has raised a large endowment, second only to Brookings among the DC-5, and its annual budget is a close second. Its wide base of donors (with numerous small contributors as well as many major supporters) is cited as key to avoiding becoming beholden to a few large sources. Heritage does not take funding from government.

With no academic pretensions, Heritage has attracted a staff of generally younger researchers who prepare analyses of the issues currently facing the Congress and the nation generally. They pride themselves on their ability to write a useful policy report in a matter of days and sometimes even hours.[28] Heritage often refers to being engaged in a "war of ideas." Early on, Heritage borrowed tactics from the large environmental organizations like the Sierra Club and launched extensive direct-mail fundraising campaigns. It also involved local organizations, especially via its Resource Bank (discussed later on).[29]

Each year Heritage produces several hundred research papers, about ten books, and hundreds of web memos. It also maintains a widely-used Web site. The organization distributes its research products to every member of Congress as well as to executive branch policy makers, journalists, academics, and the general public. In 2006, Heritage conducted over 180 issue briefings for federal government officials and its staff members testified at 28 congressional committee hearings. The organization also graduated 50 staffers from its Congressional Fellows program. Overall, Heritage sponsored 178 lectures and seminars in 2006 and its staff wrote over 1,000 op-ed essays which appeared in newspapers around the country.[30]

Table 3.4
Highlights of Heritage Foundation

Headquarters
214 Massachusetts Avenue NE
Washington, DC 20002

Date Founded: 1973

Official Purpose

To formulate and promote conservative public policies based on the principles of free enterprise, limited government, individual freedom, traditional American values, and a strong national defense

Main Areas of Focus

Foreign Policy
Economic and Political Thought
Budget and Taxation
Education, Health, and Welfare

Size of Staff

Approximately 200

Leadership

CEO: Edwin Feulner

Some Key Research Staff

Stuart Butler, Domestic Policy
Daniel Mitchell, Economic Policy

Government

21 member Board of Trustees

Revenues and Expenses in 2005

Operating revenues:	$40.0 million
Operating expenditures:	$36.5 million
(Development	$5.0 million)

Source: Heritage Foundation (annual reports and other documents).

Heritage is invariably described as a conservative think tank. It states bluntly that it believes in limited government, a strong national defense, and traditional American values. In the words of Edwin Feulner, its long-term president, "Everyone at Heritage works from a common policy perspective."[31] As the holder of a Wharton MBA, Feulner attempts to run a business-like think tank, while serving as its CEO. It also has been observed that the Heritage staff tends to resemble that of a congressional office more than that of the more academically inclined research institutions whose reputation is based in large measure on academic publications.[32]

Heritage's quality control appears to be less structured than AEI or Brookings. For most studies, the key reviews of the substance and accuracy are made internally by the leaders of the research effort. However, in the case of the economic modeling program, outside reviewers are relied upon to ensure that the results reflect the current state of the art.[33]

One of the most impressive evaluations of Heritage's impact on the Washington-based think tank community comes from Karlyn Bowman, a long-term member of AEI's staff: "The Heritage Foundation's emergence on the think tank scene in 1974 changed the way all think tanks in Washington do business." Bowman went on to state, "Think tanks were pretty sleepy places until this scrappy, energetic new organization arrived."[34]

Cato Institute

The newest of the five think tanks is the Cato Institute (see Table 3-5). It prides itself on its libertarian orientation and its departure from the conventional wisdom. The organization is named for Cato's Letters, a series of libertarian pamphlets that helped to lay the philosophical foundation for the American Revolution. Cato attempts to combine an appreciation for entrepreneurship, the market process, and lower taxes with strict respect for civil liberties and skepticism about the benefits of the welfare state and "military adventurism."[35]

Cato states that it "seeks to broaden the parameters of public policy debate to allow consideration of the traditional American principles of limited government, individual liberty, free markets, and peace." It claims to lead "the battle to protect free trade." Cato relies primarily on support from more than 15,000 individuals, as well as a variety of foundations. In the fiscal year ending March 31, 2007, Cato received only 3 percent of its income from corporations. It does not accept any government funding.

Table 3.5
Highlights of Cato Institute

Headquarters
1000 Massachusetts Avenue NW
Washington, DC 20001

Date Founded: 1977

Official Purpose
To broaden public policy debates consistent with the traditional American principles
of individual liberty, limited government, dynamic market capitalism, and peaceful
relations among nations

Main Areas of Focus
Trade Policy
Defense and Foreign Policy
Fiscal Policy
Natural Resources

Size of Staff
About 100 full-time employees, 90 adjunct scholars and fellows plus interns

Leadership
CEO: Edward H. Crane

Some Key Staff
William Niskanen, Economics
Roger Pilon, Legal Policy
Dan Griswold, International Trade Policy
Chris Edwards, Tax Policy
Ted Galen Carpenter, Foreign Policy

Governance
14 member Board of Directors

Revenues and Expenses in 2005
Revenues: $22.5 million
Expenses: $17.2 million
(Development $2.1 million)

Source: Cato Institute (annual reports and numerous other documents).

Cato is invariably identified as conservative when viewed in the traditional liberal-conservative spectrum.[36] However, the organization does not feel comfortable with any of the conventional labels—conservative, classical liberal, or liberal. When pressed, it prefers the term "market liberal" to describe its intellectual approach to public policy. Most of its researchers are young and highly motivated to focus on current public policy issues, although some senior staff members have strong scholarly backgrounds. Its staff operates from a "framework of Cato ideological views."[37]

The organization's target audience consists of "intermediaries" between formal decision-makers and policy analysts—primarily staffs on Capitol Hill and in the administration as well as journalists. Cato's Forum Series on the Hill provided sixteen briefings in 2006, which attracted many congressional staff members and sometimes also members of Congress. It also launched in 2006 the first Cato University on Capitol Hill, designed to provide younger Capitol Hill staffers with an understanding of the principles that underlie its libertarian policy proposals.

Cato is in an experimental mode, trying a variety of ways to communicate the analyses effectively. For example, it has discontinued its own TV and radio shows because of low levels of response but is now emphasizing use of the Internet. Cato's Web site reports more than 30,000 visits on a typical workday. New efforts include online weekly videos and an online monthly magazine, in addition to daily podcasts. To reach audiences overseas, Cato maintains Web sites in Russian, Arabic, and Spanish. It distributes copies of the U.S. Constitution on these overseas Web sites as well as through its domestic activities.

Cato relies primarily on an internal review group to provide quality control of its research reports. Its Policy Committee meets monthly to evaluate proposed studies. For the *Cato Journal*, it uses outside reviewers as well as its own experts. Chairman William Niskanen states that the quality of the organization's research is reflected in the fact that more outside experts have become interested in taking on Cato-sponsored research assignments.[38]

The organization hosts about 200 events a year, covering a wide variety of domestic and international issues where its researchers can interact with representatives of government, interest groups, journalists, and other think tanks. Like Brookings and AEI, Cato publishes a wide variety of books on domestic and international topics as well as shorter reports on current issues (44 policy studies in 2006) and numerous "op-eds" in major newspapers (358 in 2006). Table 3-6 shows some highlights of Cato's varied activities in one week in November 2006.

Table 3.6
A Week in the Life of the Cato Institute, November 12-17, 2006

SUNDAY	MONDAY	TUESDAY	WEDNESDAY	THURSDAY	FRIDAY
New York Post reviews Cato book on income and wealth.	Cato foreign policy analyst addresses annual meeting of Citizens for Global Solutions in D.C.	Cato holds conference in New York City. Speakers include Senator Chuck Hagel (R-Nebr.)	Cato staffer debates energy policy with Sierra Club on CNBC-TV.	Cato hosts annual monetary policy conference. Speakers include a governor of Federal Reserve Board, President of St. Louis Fed, and Harvard University economics professor.	Cato officer speaks at Federalist Society National convention.
Washington Times runs op-ed by author.	Cato analyst defends school choice in debate at Americans United for Separation of Church and State.	Cato tax forum in D.C. features former deputy prime minister of Slovakia.	Cato staffer meets with Chinese delegation on trade policy.	Cato staffer addresses Federalist Society National Convention.	Cato hosts author of book on a biblical case for legal toleration.
Chicago Sun-Times runs op-ed on foreign policy.	Cato researcher briefs CNBC-TV host who will interview Robert Redford on global warming.	Cato staffer speaks at Tennessee Center for Policy Research in Nashville.	Cato analyst speaks at George Mason University.	Cato editor lectures high school students at YMCA Youth & Government Program.	Cato official is interviewed by *New York Times* on global warming.
		Cato economist briefs Oregon senator on tax reform.	Cato analyst speaks at policy roundtable of America's Future Foundation.		
			Cato analyst speaks at Cornell University on health care.		
			Cato analyst lectures at Texas A&M University on trade policy.		

Source: Cato Policy Report, January/February 2007, pp. 6-7.

General Observation

Each of the DC-5 plays an important and special role in the public policy arena in the nation's capital. The chapters that follow try to analyze their overall contribution, positive and negative, and to make some comparisons among them.

Notes

1. James G. McGann, "Academics to Ideologues: A Brief History of the Public Policy Research Industry," *P.S.: Political Science and Politics*, December 1992, p. 736.
2. James Allen Smith, *The Idea Brokers: Think Tanks and the Rise of the New Policy Elite* (New York: Free Press, 1991); Donald E. Abelson, *A Capitol Idea: Think Tanks and U.S. Foreign Policy* (Montreal: McGill-Queens University Press, 2006); James G. McGann and R. Kent Weaver, editors, *Think Tanks and Civil Societies* (New Brunswick, NJ: Transaction Publishers, 2000); Andrew Rich, *Think Tanks, Public Policy, and the Politics of Expertise* (Cambridge: Cambridge University Press, 2004); David M. Ricci, *The Transformation of American Politics: The New Washington and the Rise of Think Tanks* (New Haven: Yale University Press, 1993).
3. "About Brookings," The Brookings Institution (www.brookings/edu/index/about.htm). "Brookings was the first independent organization dedicated exclusively to conducting public policy research," James G. McGann, "Academics to Ideologues: A Brief History of the Public Policy Research Industry," *P.S.: Political Science and Politics*, December 1992, p. 733.
4. Alice Rivlin, "Policy Analysis at the Brookings Institution," in Carol H. Weiss, ed., *Organizations for Policy Analysis* (Newbury Park, CA: Sage Publications, 1992), p. 22.
5. Donald E. Abelson, *A Capitol Idea: Think Tanks and U.S. Foreign Policy* (Montreal: McGill-Queens University Press, 2006), p. 160. Attempting to get media coverage is hardly a recent development on the part of Washington-based public policy research institutes. In 1916, the Institute for Government Research (one of the three interrelated organizations that were combined to form the Brookings Institution) hired a public relations specialist to place editorials and articles supporting the establishment of a national budget system in major newspapers throughout the United States (Abelson, p. 61).
6. Sidney Blumenthal, *The Rise of the Counter-Establishment* (New York: Times Books, 1986), p. 38.
7. Strobe Talbott, "The Role of Independent Research in Partisan Times," *Vital Speeches of the Day*, May 2006, p. 439.
8. Robert J. Samuelson, "Making the Think Tanks Think," *Washington Post*, August 1, 2007, p. A17.
9. Interview with Tom Mann, Brookings Institution, Washington, DC, July 17, 2007.
10. Interview with William Antholis, Brookings Institution, Washington, DC, July 18, 2007.
11. Stuart M. Butler, *Evolving Beyond Traditional Employer-Sponsored Health Insurance*, The Hamilton Project Discussion Paper 2007-06 (Washington, DC: Brookings Institution, 2007).
12. Jenny Anderson, "Scrutiny on Tax Rates That Fund Managers Pay," *New York Times*, June 13, 2007, p. C-3; see also Brookings Institution, *The Hamilton Project*, June 14, 2007.

13.   Author's interview with William Antholis, Brookings Institution, Washington, DC, July 18, 2007.

14.   Brookings Institution, *Annual Report 2006* (Washington, DC: Brookings Institution, 2006), pp. 8, 11.

15.   Robert J. Samuelson, "Making the Think Tanks Think," *Washington Post*, August 1, 2007, p. A17.

16.   "AEI's Organization and Purposes," American Enterprise Institute for Public Policy Research (www.aei.org/about).

17.   Donald E. Abelson, *A Capitol Idea: Think Tanks and U.S. Foreign Policy* (Montreal: McGill-Queens University Press, 2006), p. 81.

18.   Based on the author's interview with Christopher DeMuth, President of AEI, Washington, DC, January 21, 2007.

19.   "About CSIS," Center for Strategic and International Studies (www.csis.org/about).

20.   Interview with Dr. John Hamre, President of CSIS, Washington, DC, May 9, 2007.

21.   James Kitfield, "CSIS Embraces Old Mission With New Faces," *National Journal*, September 9, 2000, p. 2807.

22.   "Think Tanks: Who's Hot and Who's Not," *The International Economy*, Summer 2005.

23.   Stanley Foundation, *Policy Dialogue Brief*, November 2006, pp. 1-12.

24.   James Allen Smith, *The Idea Brokers: Think Tanks and the Rise of the New Policy Elite* (New York: Free Press, 1991).

25.   Zbigniew Brzezinski, *Second Chance, Three Presidents and the Crisis of American Superpower* (New York: Basic Books, 2007), p. 217.

26.   Donald E. Abelson, *A Capitol Idea: Think Tanks and U.S. Foreign Policy* (Montreal: McGill-Queens University Press, 2006), p. 92.

27.   "About the Heritage Foundation," The Heritage Foundation (www.heritage.org/about/).

28.   Lee Edwards, *The Power of Ideas: The Heritage Foundation at 25 Years* (Ottawa, IL: Jameson Books, 1997), p. 37.

29.   Leslie R. Crutchfield and Heather McLeod Grant, *Forces for Good* (San Francisco: Jossey-Bass, 2008), p. 93.

30.   *2006 Annual Report* (Washington, DC: Heritage Foundation, 2007), p. 30.

31.   Edwin Feulner, "The Heritage Foundation," in McGann and Weaver, *Think Tanks and Civil Societies*, p. 73.

32.   James Allen Smith, *The Idea Brokers: Think Tanks and the Rise of the New Policy Elite* (New York: Free Press, 1991), p. 205.

33.   Author's interview with Edwin Feulner, President of Heritage Foundation, Washington, DC, October 25, 2007.

34.   Joe Rogalsky, "Edwin Feulner," *The Examiner*, October 1, 2007, p. 13.

35.   "About Cato," Cato Institute (www.cato.org/about/about.html).

36.   Robert J. Samuelson, "Making the Think Tanks Think," *Washington Post*, August 1, 2007, p. A17.

37.   Author's interview with Cato President Ed Crane, Washington, DC, June 19, 2007. See also Cato Institute, *2006 Annual Report* (Washington, DC: 2007).

38.   Author's interview with Dr. William Niskanen, Washington, DC, June 19, 2007. See also Cato Institute, *2006 Annual Report*.

4

Making Some Comparisons

Each one of the DC-5 has experienced significant ebbs and flows in its effectiveness—and often in its ability to attract financial support. Nevertheless, unlike most other think tanks, the DC-5 as a group have been influential in a variety of important public policy issues over a considerable period of time. Because of their visibility and stature in the policy-making community, they enjoy unusually close ties with important policymakers and with major media outlets. Many of their senior scholars regularly exchange ideas, formally or informally, with senior members of the executive and legislative branches.[1]

Examining the Numbers

It is useful to begin a comparison of the five think tanks by looking at their finances. Table 4.1 presents recent data on key measures of inputs or resources available to and used by the five think tanks analyzed here. It is clear that, in financial terms, Brookings has by far the largest pool of assets and, by smaller margins, the most annual revenues and annual expenditures. However, according to the data in Chapter 3, its full-time staff is smaller than either Heritage or AEI. Each of the five organizations also has part-time researchers, but to varying degrees. Although many of these numbers may look absolutely large, they are dwarfed by the size of governmental statistical bureaus or faculties of the major universities.

Moreover, the financial trends of the DC-5 have not followed a straight line. For example, AEI has rebounded from near bankruptcy in 1986. Its net assets (reserves and endowment) now could cover more than twice its annual expenditures. Comparable calculations for Brookings and Heritage are higher—five times and three times, respectively. Cato's net assets could cover one year of outlays. While CSIS closely balances income and outlay each year; it has embarked on a major effort to generate a substantial endowment.

Table 4.1
Finances of Five Major Think Tanks
(In millions of dollars in 2005)

Think Tank	Revenues	Expenditures	Net Assets
AEI	37.9	21.5	69.3
Brookings	47.7	39.7	269.7
Cato	22.5	17.2	21.1
CSIS	27.2	27.1	34.4
Heritage	43.9	36.5	137.3

Source: Financial statements of the five think tanks.

Contrary to a widely held impression, none of the five think tanks relies primarily on business funding. It is interesting to note the variation among the five major think tanks in their dependence on the various sources of funding (see Table 4.2). For example, Cato and Heritage rely primarily on individuals for their annual finances—83 percent in the case of Cato and 59 percent for Heritage. The result is that many of their supporters make small contributions on the basis of general mail solicitations. As shown in Table 4.3, that entails devoting a significantly higher portion of annual expenditures to fundraising than is the case in the other three think tanks.

In contrast AEI receives the bulk of its funds (58 percent) from a combination of generous individual and corporate supporters. In the case of CSIS, foundations and corporations provide a clear majority of the funds (63 percent). Brookings depends much more heavily on its endowment than any of the other DC-5. The draw from the endowment, 25 percent of total revenues, is the largest single source of its annual income.

The attitudes of both fans and critics of the think tank phenomenon are formed by examining their financing as well as many other factors. Some observers view the special strength of independently-financed think tanks as providing an alternative source of policy information to that presented by government and as a potential critic of government policy.[2] However, other analysts seem to reflect the mirror image of that viewpoint. They are concerned that the substantial private sector support of the think tanks may bias them at times to adopt the positions of "special interests." That surely is a viewpoint that deserves to be considered. For example, one recent critic simply states that "the American Enterprise Institute . . . has long been the reliable voice of corporate money."[3]

Table 4.2, however, provides evidence for a different viewpoint. Like the other conservative think tanks, AEI receives a limited portion (21 percent) of its funds from corporations. In fact, a key reason to downplay the concern that an interest group may come to dominate the work of one of the major think tanks is the great variety of the sources of their financing, including companies that normally compete against each other both in the marketplace and in the public policy arena.

For example, retail firms and manufacturing companies tend to have sharply different views on the question of relying heavily on taxation of sales versus taxation on income and profits. Likewise, in a given industry, firms that export substantially are more likely to oppose restrictions on international trade than companies facing strong competition from imports. As shown in a later chapter, often the key concerns of a business supporter of a think tank relate to more practical matters than trying to influence its statements on broad issues of public policy.

Some Qualitative Comparisons

Despite important overall similarities in the operations of the DC-5, substantial differences are visible among them—and have been recognized by a variety of scholars. For example, even though all of them have published studies on tax policy, Brookings scholars show more interest in the effect of taxes on the distribution of income ("fairness" concerns) while AEI, Cato, and Heritage research tends to focus more on the

Table 4.2
Revenue Sources of Five Major Think Tanks
Percentage Distribution in 2005

Think Tank	Individuals	Corporations	Foundations	Government	Endowment Income	Conferences Sales, etc.
AEI	37	21	16	0	0	26
Brookings	20	17	19	2	25	17
Cato	83	2	11	0	0	4
CSIS	12	28	35	9	5	11
Heritage	59	5	24	0	8	4

Source: Financial statements of the five think tanks (Brookings data based in part on discussion with a Brookings administrator).

Table 4.3
Allocation of Expenditures by DC-5 in 2005
(percentage distribution)

Organization	Program Services	Management and General	Fundraising	Total
AEI	82	14	4	100
Brookings	75	19	6	100
Cato	66	20	14	100
CSIS	72	21	7	100
Heritage	83	3	14	100

Source: IRS Forms 990, "Return of Organization Exempt From Income Tax," 2005.

influence of tax policy on the incentives to work, save, and invest ("efficiency" concerns). Reflecting its orientation to international relations, the more modest amount of work on tax policy performed by CSIS is geared to strengthening the economic position of the United States in its dealings with other nations.[4]

There also are great differences in the professional prominence of their staffs. In 2006, ten members of the senior staffs of the DC-5 were Fellows of the American Academy of Arts and Sciences. Six were affiliated with Brookings, and two each with AEI and CSIS.[5] AEI and Brookings over the years have drawn to their research staffs several former presidents of the American Economic Association (luminaries such as Arthur Okun, Charles Schultze, William Fellner, and Gottfried Haberler). Cato and Heritage, in contrast, recruit a larger proportion of younger researchers, often those who do not hold a doctorate degree.

Likewise, the public policy experiences of the staff vary widely. The CSIS roster includes former Secretaries of State (such as Henry Kissinger) and Defense (such as Harold Brown) while AEI has a former Speaker of the House of Representatives (Newt Gingrich). Heritage hosts a former Attorney General (Edwin Meese) and Cato a former acting chairman of the Council of Economic Advisers (William Niskanen).

There are many dimensions on which the DC-5 can be compared. A Harris poll conducted in November 2006 reported that 73 percent of the American public trusted the Brookings Institution, compared to 68 percent for the Heritage Foundation and 58 percent for the Cato Institute (these were the only think tanks covered in the survey). It is fascinating to note that Republicans had a higher degree of confidence in all three think tanks than did Democrats. However, Heritage outranked Brookings in the absolute rankings among Republicans, by 84 percent to 77 percent.[6]

Although there is considerable ideological variation within most of the think tanks, each has developed a distinct public image. Cato is considered to be libertarian, Heritage and AEI conservative, Brookings liberal, and CSIS bipartisan. Moreover, there is great variety in the balance that each of the five groups strikes between research and advocacy. Individual researchers in all of the think tanks present their personal views to congressional bodies and media representatives, but the allocation of time to such activity ranges from relatively low at Brookings to relatively high at Heritage.

The complexity that exists in the Washington think tank community is also illustrated by the significant efforts made to sponsor joint endeavors. Despite the inherent rivalry among the DC-5 and with other think tanks, the following significant joint efforts were reported in 2006-2007:

1. Two major joint centers continue to flourish: the AEI-Brookings Joint Center for Regulatory Studies and the Brookings-Urban Institute Joint Center on Tax Policy.
2. Several books on public policy have been jointly produced, including: *Competitive Equity*, by Peter Wallison (AEI) and Robert Litan (Brookings), and *China: The Balance Sheet*, by scholars at CSIS and the Peterson Institute for International Economics.
3. In 2006, CSIS joined with the Baker Institute at Rice University and the Center for the Study of the Presidency to serve as sponsoring organizations of the Iraq Study Group co-chaired by James Baker and Lee Hamilton.
4. A joint assessment of the No Child Left Behind Act was presented at AEI in November 2006 by staff of AEI and the Thomas B. Fordham Foundation.
5. In 2006, experts from Brookings and Heritage joined forces with the Concord Coalition and the U.S. Government Accountability Office to conduct a "Fiscal Wake-Up" tour covering eleven major cities. The combined group met with editorial boards, business leaders, academics, and citizen organizations in an effort to alert the American public about the nation's long-term fiscal problems. Especial attention was given on how to finance the federal government's three major entitlement programs—Medicare, Medicaid, and social security.[7]

A somewhat different example of joint efforts is provided by the Pew Charitable Trusts. In 2007, the Pew Mobility project involved researchers from AEI, Brookings, Heritage, and the Urban Institute. However, the overall project responsibility was lodged in the Pew organizations, rather than in the think tanks. The project's first report, released in May

2007, showed that American men in their thirties today are economically worse off than their fathers' generation. This is a sharp reversal from a long-time trend visible as recently as a decade ago, showing continuous improvement in family income over time.[8]

A later section of this book (Chapter 7) presents a more detailed analysis of the actual influence that the major think tanks exert on the public policy process. However, on the basis of the material in this and the preceding chapter, some initial observations can be offered.

Preliminary Thoughts on the Work of the DC-5

In terms of the cumulative impact of think tanks on public policy, there is great variation in the case of specific issues as well as of public perception. On some issues and on selected occasions, a more specialized think tank—one, say, focusing mainly on foreign affairs (such as the Council on Foreign Relations) or taxation (the Tax Foundation or the Institute for Research on the Economics of Taxation)—may receive more attention. On other occasions, a university-based research group such as Stanford's Hoover Institution or even an individual faculty member specializing in monetary policy (the distinguished economist Milton Friedman quickly comes to mind) may have a greater impact. In terms of the desires of specific constituencies, a more narrowly focused organization may be a more relevant mechanism for promoting its views on certain issues. Thus, at times, an interest group directly representing labor (the AFL-CIO) or business (the national Chamber of Commerce) or another segment of society (AARP or the National Rifle Association)—or a for-profit research firm—may be most influential in a particular circumstance.

Nevertheless, judged by their overall performance over recent decades, the DC-5 are looked upon by government officials, the media, and interest groups as important continuing sources of information on and analysis of a wide array of current and often very controversial issues facing the nation. One long-time DC-based reporter says that the most useful think tanks have smart, knowledgeable people who can put the breaking news into context.[9]

All of the five think tanks—and many others—realize that the long-term effectiveness of their activities depends on the confidence in the integrity as well as the relevance of their work. Although the researchers in each of the organizations often hold well-known views on specific controversial matters, they are generally respected for the accuracy of the data they present and the professionalism of their analyses. As a practical matter, it would be very harmful to the future role of a Washington think tank if a member of Congress were embarrassed because he or she used a think tank's information, which turned out to be wrong.

Each of the think tanks has a unique intellectual environment. Although classifications are inherently arbitrary, it is tempting to distinguish between a "top-down" point of view epitomized by Heritage and Cato with the "bottom up" approach on the part of Brookings and CSIS, with AEI located somewhere in between.

Of course, we should not push this dichotomy too far. Nobody stands over a Heritage or Cato researcher, dictating to them what to say or write. Likewise, I have not come across a Marxist or a nihilist at the other think tanks. All that is due to the fact that the key point of control or influence over think tank staff members is the power of the management to hire them in the first place.

An important and unappreciated factor is the feedback effect resulting from the informal interaction among the staffs of the five organizations. They often speak at each other's meetings (sometimes that encounter may be in debate format), write for each other's publications, and participate in each other's public meetings. They also read and comment on, in public or in private, each other's research and publications. This interaction provides an important but informal type of quality control. Thus, even while competing for public attention, Dr. X at Tank A wants to keep the professional respect of Dr. Y at Tank B—and vice versa. They both may have received their graduate degrees from the same university or served on the same governmental advisory committee!

Each of the five think tanks has faced a variety of internal as well as external challenges over the years—ranging from problems in recruiting and motivating a very special staff of "thinkers" to raising large amounts of funds for an organization generating extremely intangible outputs. The DC-5, both as a group and individually, has met these challenges and, at present, each continues on a growth trajectory.

Appendix: A Note on Other Think Tanks

It is estimated that approximately 1,400 think tanks exist in the United States.[10] That number covers a variety of sizes, activities, and locations and includes many university-affiliated research institutes. The visible success of the major Washington-based think tanks has encouraged the formation of state and regional organizations as well as many specialized groups, both in the United States and overseas.

Since the end of the Cold War, hundreds of think tanks have been established in previous communist nations, in addition to a considerable number that have existed in Western Europe and East Asia for a considerable period of time.

The American think tank model, characterized by very strong independence, has generally served as the standard for the newer overseas organizations. However, this is not a universal situation. Quite a few of the more recently established public policy research institutes follow the continental European model where think tanks are aligned with political parties or business associations.[11] The Konrad-Adenauer-Stiftung, affiliated with the Christian Democratic Party of Germany, and the Herbert-Quandt-Stiftung, sponsored by the Foundation of ALTANA AG, are representative examples.

The Limited Coverage of This Analysis

It would not be practical for one researcher to attempt to analyze the activities of the total array of think tanks or even the 1,400 located in the United States. For a variety of reasons such as location outside of Washington, DC, these organizations typically do not participate in the day-to-day decision-making process in which U.S. national policy is developed. Most of them are small and focus on a single state, region, or policy issue. For example, the State Policy Network consists of over 80 independent small and mid-sized think tanks who sponsor research and/or perform activist roles in public policy in 42 states. Many of these organizations are also members of the Atlas Network sponsored by the Atlas Economic Research Foundation. That foundation helps newer market-oriented think tanks obtain initial financing and learn from the experiences of other members of the Network.[12]

As shown in Chapter 2, the emphasis on the DC-5 excludes many important public policy institutes. Focusing on five major think tanks, as is done here, is not meant to denigrate the importance of other organizations, both in Washington, DC, and elsewhere. These other organizations are excluded from the body of this study for a variety of special and cogent reasons. Many important think tanks are not covered because they are far more specialized than the five broad-gauged organizations that are the subject of this chapter.

For example, Resources for the Future (RFF) is a highly regarded Washington-based private non-profit research organization. However, unlike the five think tanks covered here, its work is limited to the areas of environmental and energy policy. Moreover, RFF does not make the effort of the five organizations to involve its staff in the nitty gritty of the public policy process. Other important and well-regarded but specialized

Washington-based think tanks include the Urban Institute, the Peterson Institute for International Economics, and the Carnegie Endowment for International Peace.

Unlike most other Washington-based think tanks, the Urban Institute receives the majority of its funding from government agencies. Although well funded from private sources, the Aspen Institute has only recently moved to the Washington area and, at least so far, has not established the wide-ranging participation in the public policy process as is character-ized by each of the DC-5.

Many others are left out because of their relatively modest size and/or newness to the Washington scene. Examples include the Center on Bud-get and Policy Priorities, the Center for the Study of the Presidency, the Economic Policy Institute, the Institute for Policy Studies, the Progress and Freedom Foundation, and the Progressive Policy Institute. It should be noted that these omitted think tanks range from the far right to the far left, with several usually considered middle-of-the-road.

The Woodrow Wilson International Center for Scholars is not listed because of its tie to the Smithsonian Institution and also because the organization per se maintains a considerable detachment from the public policy process. Other important think tanks are omitted from this study because they are not located in the Washington area and thus do not partici-pate in the informal but vital daily interaction with the Washington-based policy community. That physical detachment from the Washington scene may, on occasion, provide for a greater degree of independence than those that are caught up in the daily interactions of the Washington policy com-munity. A key example is the Hoover Institution, located on the West Coast. Unlike freestanding think tanks, Hoover is also affiliated with a major university, Stanford. Another example is the Levy Economic Institute of Bard College located in Annandale-on-Hudson in New York State.

Similarly, the National Bureau of Economic Research is omitted be-cause it is located in Massachusetts. On occasion, the reports of this major non-profit economic research organization receive substantial attention from decision makers. Consistent with its academic orientation, however, the National Bureau does not typically involve itself in the public policy process of testifying before congressional committees, briefing com-mittee staffs, and encouraging interviews with the media. The Century Foundation, located in New York City, concentrates on funding important policy-oriented research much of which is performed elsewhere.

The Council for Foreign Relations is omitted, although it has an important Washington presence, because its headquarters location is in

New York.[13] Admittedly, this is a close call. The Council's report for 2006 boasts that its staff testified 15 times before congressional committees, conducted more than 150 briefings for executive branch officials and members of Congress (including breakfasts with new members of Congress), gave "countless" media interviews, and wrote more than 200 op-eds.

To cite a few other examples of organizations omitted from this study, the Foreign Policy Research Institute specializes in issues of international relations and is located in Pennsylvania. The Manhattan Institute, focusing on urban and other domestic policy issues, is situated in New York City. The Hudson Institute is headquartered in Indiana, albeit with a significant Washington office. The Rand Corporation is not covered in view of the major financial support it receives from government agencies and its primary location on the West Coast.

Still others are not included in this analysis because they tend to focus more on advocacy than research. Examples include the Competitive Enterprise Institute (CEI) and Freedom Works (formerly Citizens for a Sound Economy). On its website, Freedom Works reports 800,000 "grass roots volunteers." In North Carolina, two Freedom Works county chapters helped to defeat two tax increases. Freedom Works activists led phone banks and wrote letters demanding that their taxes not be raised.[14]

Notes

1.   James G. McGann, "How Think Tanks Are Coping With the Future," *The Futurist*, November/December 2000, p. 16.
2.   Donald E. Abelson, *A Capital Idea: Think Tanks and U.S. Foreign Policy* (Montreal: McGill-Queens University Press, 2006), p. xiv.
3.   Thomas Frank, "Thus Spake Zinsmeister," *New York Times*, August 25, 2006, p. A23.
4.   *Strengthening America* (Washington, DC: Center for Strategic and International Studies, 1992).
5.   *Bulletin of the American Academy of Arts and Sciences*, Fall 2006, pp. 80-87, 94, 95.
6.   Brookings Institution, *Quality, Independence, Impact: A Reputation by the Numbers* (Washington, DC: Brookings Institution, undated), p. 1. See also Jim Grote, "Extreme Philanthropy," *Financial Planning*, October 2007, p. 82.
7.   *2006 Annual Report* (Washington, DC: Heritage Foundation, 2007), p. 11.
8.   Greg Ip, "Not Your Father's Pay: Why Wages Today Are Weaker," *Wall Street Journal*, May 25, 2007, p. A2.
9.   Personal experience of the author bolstered by interview with an experienced Washington journalist, July 2, 2007.
10.   James G. McGann, *2007 Survey of Think Tanks: A Summary Report* (Philadelphia: August 2007).
11.   Raymond J. Struyk, *Managing Think Tanks* (Washington, DC: Urban Institute, 2002).

12.   Atlas Economic Research Foundation, *Year in Review Fall 2006.*

13.   CFR chairman Peter G. Peterson stated in late 2006 that the organization desired to secure its own building in Washington, DC, "to reaffirm our position there as both the leading foreign policy think tank and convener." See "The Council Celebrates 85 Years." *The CFR Chronicle*, November 2006, p. 3. In September 2007, Council President Richard N. Haas described the level of the organization's activity in Washington as "nearly the same as in New York." *The CFR Chronicle*, September 2007, p. 1.

14.   "National," *SPN News*, July/August 2007, p. 19.

5

How Think Tanks Operate

The fundamental attraction—and impact—of the Washington-based think tanks has been described succinctly by David Ricci, an astute observer of the phenomenon:

> Power in Washington cannot be measured precisely, yet think tanks surely have a good deal of it, in a city where tens of thousands of consultants, journalists, lobbyists…and other policy-minded people spend most of their working time trying to influence the course of government decisions.[1]

Power and influence are inherently subjective aspects of human relationships.[2] Analysts invariably find the effort to measure these phenomena filled with frustration. As noted in Chapter 1, it is rare that any individual think tank exercises an important role in every step in the public policy process in the case of any single public policy issue. Yet, virtually every observer of the think tank phenomenon agrees that the total impact of the efforts of the DC-5 is substantial. In this chapter, we examine how those very specialized organizations actually function.

Sorting Out the Activities of Think Tanks

Each of the major think tanks (as well as many other Washington-based public policy research organizations) conduct five major and interrelated functions:

1. Think tanks continually research and analyze public policy issues. The work of their extensive staffs encompasses a wide array of subject matter, domestic and international, political, social, and economic. In doing so, they employ a range of research methodologies, formal and informal, controversial and mainstream. Their research and analysis range from year-long projects to develop innovative solutions to societal problems to quickly prepared appraisals of current policy proposals. As one analyst has described this phenomenon, though often portrayed as organizations of experts engaged in quiet contemplation, think tanks are "a hub of activity."[3]

Nevertheless, one very knowledgeable veteran of the Washington scene described to the author an important limitation to the effectiveness of think tanks: in his opinion, some of these organizations do not really understand the importance of accommodating good policy proposals with the real world constraints that face policy makers.[4] On that score there is great variation within and across the major think tanks.

2. Think tanks often "outsource" research and establish networks for specific projects. Any major think tank is a complex organization. Often a large project will be conducted by means of a temporary "network" organization. The project leader may not necessarily reside at the think tank. He or she may be a faculty member housed at a university hundreds of miles away. Although I have never encountered the term "outsourcing" being used in this connection at any think tank, these organizations surely do a great deal of it.

Those who serve on a think tank research team, in addition to full-time members of the think tank staff, may also be located at a variety of non-profit institutions and on occasion at a few large corporations or other for-profit firms. Although not a permanent organization, the successful network may influence the way future projects at the organization are structured and staffed.

Universities as well as independent research institutes have been using such a networking approach far longer than the current wave of business outsourcing in the United States. In the early 1960s, Emile Benoit of Columbia University and Kenneth Boulding of the University of Michigan co-directed a pioneering research effort on the economics of disarmament. Individual researchers were located at Columbia University, George Washington University, Harvard University, New York University, Research Analysis Corporation, Standard Oil (NJ), Stanford Research Institute, Townsend-Greenspan Co., the University of Colorado, the University of Illinois, the University of Michigan, and the U.S. Council of Economic Advisers.[5]

From the viewpoint of the project sponsor, networks can be very cost-effective as they obviate the need to maintain on the permanent staff experts whose special contributions are only required on special occasions. Moreover, in this manner a think tank can pull in for limited periods of time outstanding authorities who cannot be lured to leave their organizational home, be it a university or a for-profit enterprise.

All of the DC-5 "outsource" a significant part of their research; that is, they depend on people whose primary position is elsewhere to perform at times significant portions of their substantive work. However, CSIS set a high point for bringing in outsiders at its first major research undertaking in 1963. To improve communication between researchers on problems of strategy and more conventional academic areas, especially economics, the original Center for Strategic Studies commissioned thirty-four papers from individual experts at sixteen universities, five think tanks (including itself) and one corporation.[6] The work was supervised by two staff members of the Center (who comprised a large part of its in-house workforce at the time). In the case of the dozens of experts that the Center brought together for its initial 1963 conference, only two currently have offices there—Henry Kissinger and James Schlesinger. At times, however, a few other participants (including me) have been involved in specific CSIS activities.

The temporary research "network" provides great flexibility. There is no need to fire any of the outsourcers when research requirements change at the termination of a specific project; the relationship simply dissolves—unless it is renewed for another project and often with a different time or subject commitment.

3. Think tanks devote very considerable effort to disseminating the results of their work. Each of the DC-5 issues a variety of publications, maintains a website, encourages its staff members to make presentations to professional and government groups, and works with the media. Their publications range from scholarly journals to short memos, with a considerable variation of reports and studies in between (see Table 5.1 for examples). Web sites are increasingly used to reach audiences rapidly and with modest incremental effort and expense. One experienced economic journalist sums up the prevailing view in the Washington press, "Think tank research is grist for my mill."[7]

Although each describes the activity a bit differently, all of the five think tanks devote substantial resources to "marketing" their output. Hundreds or even thousands of copies of an individual report are distributed, often without charge, to mailing lists of people in the public and private sectors considered to be influential or sympathetic to the organization's objectives. Great reliance is placed on "secondary distribution"—newspapers, magazines, radio and television, and the Internet—to reach audiences measured in the millions.

The coverage of an organization's views and activities in the media, especially in the major national television networks and key newspa-

Table 5.1
Representative Think Tank Publication Series

Journals

Brookings Papers on Economic Activity (Brookings)
The Cato Journal (Cato)
The Washington Quarterly (CSIS)

Magazines

America (AEI)
Regulation (Cato)

Report Series

AEI Policy Series
AEI Outlook Series
Brookings Policy Briefs
Cato's Letter
Cato Policy Reports
CSIS Insight
CSIS South Asia Monitor
Heritage Backgrounders

pers and magazines, serves two interrelated purposes. First of all, such widespread coverage is extremely helpful in getting the organization's name and message to decision makers as well as to those who influence them. Secondly, good coverage is an important way of demonstrating to financial supporters that their contributions are worthwhile. As a result, each think tank devotes a considerable portion of its staff resources to developing media contacts and to responding to the inquiries of individual journalists.

Much of the use of the output of the major Washington-based think tanks, both by journalists and government officials, results from the operation of informal networks within the policy community. Thus, an expert at Brookings on the distribution of the tax burden may receive calls from journalists and congressional staffs who were referred by a staff member of AEI. In turn, the AEI specialist on corporate taxation may respond to inquiries from media or government that resulted from suggestions by someone at Heritage, Brookings, or the Urban Institute.

Similarly, networks on government regulation generate reciprocal calls to and from AEI (say, on telecommunications issues), Brookings (on transportation regulation), Resources for the Future (on environmental matters), Heritage (on energy regulation), and Cato (on social regulation).

At times, lobbyists and other interest group representatives add to these direct think tank networks by bringing to the attention of journalists and government officials the work of individual think tank researchers that tend to support the specific policies that they are promoting. Such ancillary "distribution" of think tank output tends to be rather specialized. Business interests are more likely to encourage the use of AEI and Heritage studies than are labor unions or consumer groups. The latter more typically are interested in the output of Brookings and some of the newer and smaller think tanks.

Experienced journalists caution us not to confuse the frequency with which a think tank is cited and the impact of its research. Frequently, to show that "both sides" are covered in an article on a controversial issue, a reporter may quote two extreme positions, one on the right and the other on the left. However, the body of the article may be influenced far more by the analysis of a respected analyst at a more centrist think tank, frequently one of the DC-5.[8] Fundamentally, therefore, the presence of highly regarded scholars is essential to a think tank's influence.

4. Think tanks host numerous conferences and other meetings. One think tank executive believes that food is essential to a successful think tank. He contends that think tank breakfast, lunch, and dinner meetings provide the Washington equivalent of the traditional American dinner table, "where discussions are lively and it is okay (even preferable) to disagree."[9] In any event, food does attract attendance at think tank meetings.

Those conferences, seminars, briefing sessions, and other get-togethers serve several purposes. They provide a forum for the presentations of the work of the think tank sponsoring the event. These meetings also present a respectable place where government officials can present their views—and obtain substantial media coverage. A member of Congress, or a key staff assistant, could easily spend five very full days each week attending the think tank meetings to which "influentials" are regularly invited.

Because of the plethora of alternative meetings, think tanks try to make their sessions more attractive by inviting speakers and attendees from other think tanks, research organizations, universities, and interest groups. This competition of ideas often makes the event more desirable to potential participants than sessions devoted to the views of just one organization.

For example, in February 2005, AEI hosted a panel discussion on Congress and Islamist Terror. The major speakers were Edwin Meese of the Heritage Foundation, Thomas Mann of the Brookings Institution, and Lee Hamilton of the Woodrow Wilson International Center for Scholars. The following month, the AEI-Brookings joint regulatory center co-sponsored with Stanford University's Institute for Economic Policy a conference on telecommunications deregulation. Speakers included Thomas Hazlitt of the Manhattan Institute in addition to representatives of the three host organizations.

   5. Think tanks also provide training and education. Because their staff members have acquired specialized knowledge about the public policy process, each of the DC-5 has set up mechanisms for transmitting that valuable information to others. All of the major "tanks" provide internships though which college students or recent graduates serve as research assistants to senior staff members. Often, a formal program of lectures and seminars is developed for the organization's interns. From time to time they are also invited to attend the meetings described above (often interns assist in the preparation and conduct of these meetings, serving as "go-fers").

   These think tanks also provide briefing sessions for government officials and representatives of their supporters. Some of these organizations, notably Brookings, offer an extensive selection of short courses for which tuition is charged.

   Think tanks frequently attract faculty members of colleges and universities who want an opportunity to take a leave of absence or sabbatical from their educational institution to devote more time to policy-oriented research and to get a better understanding of the public policy process. Over the years, there is a two-way flow of economists, political scientists, and other professionals from universities to think tanks and back. That should not be surprising: the typical senior researcher at a Washington think tank holds a doctorate or other advanced degree from a major university.

   Heritage engages in a very different type of training—assisting a large variety of smaller think tanks that operate at a state or regional level. It provides, often without charge, a variety of services to these cooperating "grassroots" organizations. Assistance ranges from help with fundraising to workshops analyzing legislative proposals. Heritage's Annual Resource Bank is a two-day meeting at which think tank leaders from around the country are invited to participate.[10]

Some Useful Distinctions

Think tanks come in many shapes, sizes, and varieties. Thus, the distinction between a research institute and an advocacy organization is vague and often artificial. Rarely, if ever, do any of the major think tanks tell a researcher what specific conclusions to arrive at. Such action typically would be counterproductive, as word of such a ham-handed approach spreads throughout the Washington policy community. Rather, as noted earlier, the critical action is the selection of the research staff.

As a practical matter, economists who have served Democratic administrations in senior positions (e.g., as a member of the Council of Economic Advisers) are usually associated with the Brookings Institution. Their Republican counterparts often affiliate with the American Enterprise Institute and, in one case, the Cato Institute. That pattern has been too durable to be the result of chance. Nevertheless, each of those staff appointees retains a substantial amount of "academic freedom" (although the term is not generally used in this connection). Table 5-2 shows the political affiliation of the current leadership of the DC-5.

As far as advocacy is concerned, all think tanks are careful to avoid the legal hazard of advocating specific legislation (doing so could jeopardize their tax-exempt status). Rather, as institutions, they focus on broader programs and issues. However, they do not discourage individual staff members from presenting their personal views in congressional testimony and on many other occasions. Judging by their fundraising materials, such direct involvement in the legislative process is positively encouraged.

Alternative Ways of Looking at Think Tanks

Scholars and other analysts have developed many different perspectives for evaluating the role of think tanks. Each of these perspectives is helpful, but the think tank sector is too complex to lend itself to any single approach. Therefore, let us examine a variety of conceptual approaches. To start, we will consider three very different images of think tanks:

1. *The benign positive and scholarly self-image, as revealed in the Web sites and annual reports of each of the major Washington-based "tanks."* Often think tanks envision themselves as providing objective analyses of controversial public issues in an effort to enhance the public welfare. A typical statement is that of George David, vice chairman of the board of the Peterson Institute for International Economics (and CEO of United Technologies Corporation): "To me the glorious thing about this Institute is it is decidedly…nonpartisan.…It produces simply

first-class analysts, not biased left or right, and therefore we can really believe and rely on it."[11]

Some "tanks" are described rather favorably as "universities without students," while others are compared unfavorably to the supposedly unbiased college and university faculties. Neither description conforms to reality. Think tanks have very different motives than universities, especially in the creation of fundamental knowledge (far less emphasis) and in influencing the formation of public policy (far more). Moreover, in terms of positions on controversial issues, I have learned that individual faculty members can be as biased as their think tank counterparts. An inspection of the lists of advisers to major presidential candidates over many campaigns shows numerous college faculty members as well as a variety of think tank researchers.[12]

2. *The suspicious and basically negative views of the critics, especially the interest groups with very different public policy viewpoints, such as environmental organizations, unions, and trial lawyers.* Think tanks are seen by some observers as tools or captives of business to provide a counterweight to the high-minded governments and non-profit private organizations or NGOs (the "good guys in the white hats"). Certainly, the lists of boards of directors of the major think tanks include quite a few CEOs of large corporations and other wealthy individuals. We will examine in the next chapter the complex interactions between funding sources and think tank activities.

On various occasions, environmental groups such as Greenpeace (and others) use the generous financial backing of conservative or even middle-of-the-road think tanks as an argument against them, especially in gaining favorable media coverage. It turns out that the major environmental groups are also well financed by an impressive array of corporations, trade associations, and wealthy individuals.

3. *The muddy reality.* From this third viewpoint, nobody really represents the public interest. In my half-century of experience in public policy, we are all a collection of special and private interests. The distinguished economist Jagdish Bhagwati reminds us that John Stuart Mill observed that no general interest was ever advanced unless someone's special interest was advanced alongside it.[13] Good public policy is arrived at, not by the uncritical adoption of the positions of a self-proclaimed "white hat," but by the competitive give-and-take among all of the interest groups in the marketplace of ideas.

Emphasizing this last rather practical and arguably cynical approach, let us try to develop some generalizations about the roles of think tanks.

Table 5.2
Background of Think Tank Leaders

Think Tank	Individual	Current Position	Government Position	Administration or Party
Brookings	Strobe Talbott	President	Deputy Secretary of State	Clinton
AEI	Christopher DeMuth	President	OMB official	Reagan
CSIS	John Hamre	President	Deputy Secretary of Defense	Clinton
Heritage	Edwin Feulner	President	Capitol Hill staff	Republican
Cato	William Niskanen	Chairman	Member, CEA	Reagan

Source: Annual reports of the five think tanks.

Here, it is useful to draw on the work of Donald Abelson, a long-term analyst of these organizations. Abelson claims that think tanks possess four key characteristics:

1. *They are elite organizations that rely on their expertise and close ties to policymakers to advance the political and economic interests of their financial sponsors.* The DC-5 are a very special breed and they have developed significant relationships with policymakers and those that advise them. However, it is more accurate to state that each of them is identified with positions that attract certain types of financial sponsors and repel others (the array of supporters differs from think tank to think tank and over time). I have never come across evidence that any of the DC-5 changes its positions on issues to please financial supporters. Despite frequent but uninformed assumptions to the contrary, invariably each of the DC-5 takes positions on issues and then attracts financing, rather than the other way around.

2. *Think tanks are one of many groups in what has become a crowded marketplace of ideas.* To any experienced observer of the Washington scene, this is a very accurate if not obvious statement of reality.

3. *They play a modest role in shaping public policy, especially compared to the power and resources of government.* This too is an accurate statement of the situation. Yet that modest role at times can be strategic in its impact. Since the days of Archimedes, we have learned that leverage can be critical to the power of any individual force. As we will see in Chapter 7, at times a single researcher at a DC-based think tank can play an important part in the decision making process for passing a key new law.

4. *Think tanks have different mandates and resources.* Many factors influence the strategic choices that an individual think tank makes whether or not to get involved in the various stages of policymaking for the issues of the day. Those factors range from the organization's history and staff capability to its available resources and the opportunities that face it at any given point in time. For example, an invitation to testify at an important congressional hearing may generate a flurry of activity to prepare an opening statement, a formal submission, and the preparation of the staff member invited by the committee.

Taken as a whole, Abelson's description of think tank activity is useful. Yet, he misses a key ingredient: Numerous varieties of viewpoints are expressed and promoted in the overall think tank community. The most compelling guardian of the public interest is the fact that competition is pervasive in this portion of the non-profit sector.

CSIS President John Hamre offers yet another categorization of think tanks and related research organizations, which also reflects his extended experience in government. He sees four major categories of think tanks, with some overlapping cases: (1) architects, (2) general contractors, (3) suppliers, and (4) artisans. Brookings and AEI, according to Hamre, are "architects" that develop fundamental new ideas for public policy. He views CSIS as a "general contractor" who, drawing on ideas often generated by other organizations, develops a comprehensive approach to dealing with an important national security or other public policy issue. "Suppliers" are specialized organizations (e.g., environmental experts) that serve as subcontractors to the major think tanks. Finally, the "artisans" are individual researchers who are at think tanks, universities, or work as freelancers for the major "primes."[14]

We can note that, at least in part, this view of think tank relationships corresponds fairly closely to the standard way that the military establishment draws on the resources of the private sector. Heritage, we have seen, has a somewhat different and much more entrepreneurial view of the role of the major think tanks.

The rapid expansion in think tank activity in recent years has not occurred in a vacuum. This growth mirrors the increased complication of government action. A clean air statute, for example, contains approximately 800 pages of detail, while the regulations issued to carry out a new major tax law can be much longer. It takes a substantial amount of intellectual resources—both in government and in the private sector—to marshal the specific ideas ultimately embodied in such legislation and to develop the details of the implementing provisions.

Surely public policy research institutions constitute a varied lot. They differ in their sources of financial support, the constituencies they serve, the balance they strike between research and advocacy, the breadth of the policy questions they address, the professional prominence and the practical experience of their staffs, and their ideological orientation.

Sorting Out the Activities of Think Tanks

Because of the substantial variation of activity between and within each think tank, it is a real challenge to try to generalize about their activities. A useful starting point is to cite the position of thoughtful critics. Viewing think tanks from the radical left, Dan and Mary Ann Clawson have offered the following constructive summary:

> Think tanks are crucial to the policy formation process, providing information, ideas, and proposals to be considered by the government, the mass media, and capitalists themselves.[15]

A more academic description of the think tank world is provided by Yale political scientist David Ricci, who divides their work into two groups: long-term mobilization and short-term mobilization. As he sees it, long-term efforts include writing journal articles, monographs, and books so as to disseminate scholarly analyses to thoughtful readers on a variety of issues.[16] In that regard, think tanks serve as important conduits for the more fundamental research that is performed at universities.

Short-term mobilization of public opinion, in contrast, relies more on such "middle men" activities as participating in television talk shows and news programs, writing op-eds or regular columns for newspapers and magazines, and sponsoring a wide variety of meetings, symposia, and conferences. The latter activity provides an opportunity for guests to hear the in-house scholars—and other invited speakers—discuss the latest information and opinion. Other short-term activities include testifying before congressional committees, serving on advisory commissions, and providing informal sources of information for congressional staff members. The simultaneous expansion of Washington offices of businesses and other interest groups has added to the demand for think tank outputs.

In recent years, it seems clear that the short-term activity of think tanks has been given increased emphasis. The rise of the Heritage Foundation, with its success in generating policy materials used by members of the Congress in their current deliberations, is an important contributor to that trend. A second and closely related development reinforces that tendency to emphasize the short term: the rapid increase in the size and importance of congressional committee staffs has generated another important category of users of the output of think tanks.[17]

The rising educational levels of the members of Congress are also a factor (it is very nice to be told by the chairman of the committee before whom you are testifying that he studied your writings in graduate school!). Simultaneously interaction with the media has increased substantially. According to Alice Rivlin, "Brookings researchers…sometimes have to hide from the press to get any work done at all."[18] From my personal observations in Washington, that situation also occurs in other well-known think tanks.

In performing their various activities, think tanks also serve as important middlemen. They monitor academic research, extracting new ideas or forms of analysis that are used as a basis for public policy advice. In the process, the think tank analyst distills and simplifies academic knowledge so that the gist of it can be conveyed to an extremely busy denizen of Capitol Hill, the White House, or the National Press Club. Although in general academics are reluctant to admit it, much of that academic work would stay in the learned journals if think tanks did not help introduce those ideas into public policy debates. A key point is often overlooked in more general discussions of think tanks: the managers of think tanks know that they need to give their researchers considerable independence because their credibility depends in large measure on keeping the other players in the public policy process convinced of their intellectual independence.[19]

One special area of concern involves the movement of think tank personnel to and from government agencies.

A Benign Revolving Door

The general phenomenon of the "revolving door" in Washington has received substantial criticism—and for good reason. That phrase refers to the movement of senior officials in government back to the private interests they left behind when they entered government or to new private interests after their tour of service in government. This movement raises the possibility that these people may have made decisions while in government that benefited those special interests—and that they did so in the expectation that they would be rewarded for such activities after they leave government service.

The revolving door phenomenon is too complex for detailed treatment in this study. In the course of my government service and since, I have witnessed movements of people in these circumstances that are worrisome, but also many more shifts between the public and private sectors that are benign.

In the Washington think tank community especially there is a very extensive and constructive movement to and from government.[20] Federal recruiters find that senior think tank researchers often have similar educational attainments for senior positions as do university faculty (such as a Ph.D. from a major university) but possess more up-to-date knowledge of the policy issues that face government officials. They may also be more likely to have had an earlier stint of government service. Especially in the case of think tank staffers already working in Washington, it is easier to recruit them if they do not have to move their families and disrupt the education of their children.

The knowledge of policymaking officials that they can quickly return to the private sector gives an added degree of independence to political appointees who are on leaves of absence from think tanks or universities. In striking contrast, persons joining the federal service for full-time positions usually must resign from the companies or professional firms with which they previously were affiliated.

The benign revolving door is especially visible in the foreign policy community. Meetings of the Council on Foreign Relations in Washington, DC, for example, often are attended by members of the local think tanks as well as by officials in the Departments of Defense and State and other executive branch agencies. It is fascinating for an observer to witness the extensive personal exchanges of views and gossip.

Individual A (now at a DC think tank such as Brookings or CSIS) will be talking to his or her former colleague at government agency X. Individual B (now holding a federal foreign policy position) will be talking to the person he or she replaced who now resides in a Washington think tank. Both the government officials and the think tank scholars benefit from such knowledgeable and informed discussions. This phenomenon is a response to the situation in the business world often described as "It is very lonely at the top." That refers to the fact that it is helpful to hold a professional discussion with someone who is very knowledgeable but is neither your boss nor your subordinate.

A similar intellectual interaction occurs between government economists and their think tank counterparts. However, that interaction tends to be more limited. For example, a senior think tank scholar at Brookings formerly teaching at an Ivy League college is unlikely to treat a recent graduate now at Cato or Heritage as an intellectual equal. Then again, some bright graduate students at times can more than hold their own in discussions with senior members of their profession. That reflects more the university than the governmental background. In a university setting, junior faculty frequently challenge the established positions of their older colleagues who may reluctantly admit that this is the way that the profession advances.

Unlike the conventional revolving door, the movements of people between the federal government and think tanks rarely provide opportunities for financially benefiting private interests. Conceivably, an exception may arise in the award of research grants and contracts by government agencies. In most cases, however, a formal process of outside experts reviewing research proposals minimizes the likelihood of such adverse outcomes.

Limitations of Think Tanks

While examining the contributions of think tanks, it is also important to be aware of their limitations. Despite the impressive capability of some think tank experts, the limited resources of even the largest of such organizations can on occasion inhibit its response to an urgent issue. A department of the federal government or a Fortune 100 company, in contrast, can marshal far more staff people in a short period of time. Also, no one think tank commands true expertise across the wide spectrum of policy issues that face the society.

The Department of Commerce, in comparison, employs many more economists and statisticians than all of the Washington area think tanks combined. Similar statements can be made with reference to the number of experts on health care in the Department of Health and Human Services or the experts on educational policy and the Department of Education or national defense policy and the Department of Defense or foreign policy and the State Department or tax policy and the Treasury Department—and that does not begin to exhaust the listing of contrasts between think tanks and other major participants in the public policy process.

The relevant comparisons are more than numerical. Most of the professional policy analysts in government are permanent employees whose status and seniority are protected by law. Their counterparts in think tanks, no matter how long they work there, are not afforded similar protections. Aside from the benefit of custom and tradition, think tank staffers are subject to "at will" dismissal or, at best, termination of employment at the end of a fixed term of a few years. Thus, it is not surprising that often think tank experts move on to positions with other employers or bolster their positions (and income) with substantial consulting and other outside part-time employment.

One way for the think tanks to create a large "scale" of operations is for them to join forces on occasion. Chapters 3 and 4, we may recall, provide several examples of that phenomenon. However, such long-term institutional cooperation remains rare.

Somewhat more frequent is the joint effort on a single undertaking, such as the cooperation between CSIS and the Peterson Institution for International Economics on their study of U.S. policy toward Russia. Far more frequently, however, is the likelihood that individual scholars in the major think tanks will participate in a conference or other activity of a sister think tank.

In examining the activities of the major Washington-based think tanks, it is tempting to forget the wide variation of expertise within each of these organizations. To state the matter tersely but accurately, a retired member of Congress residing at Brookings is no more a scholarly researcher (and maybe less so) than the young recent college graduate working at Heritage. Each, however, does bring a different set of useful characteristics—substantial experience in public policy in one case and the enthusiasm and energy of youth in the other.

It is not accurate simply to pigeonhole individual think tanks into boxes labeled "universities without walls," "advocacy think tanks," etc. In each of the five major think tanks examined in this study, the careful observer will come across seriously committed scholars as well as people who enjoy being closer to the "action" of public policy decision-making. Think tank staff members who move to Washington from university positions will still find that they have to face competing pressures on the time available for their research. Rather than balancing research with teaching and serving on faculty committees, think tank analysts have to allocate their time between research and dealing with government officials, journalists, and other important users of their work.

Many academics have a sour view of the Washington-based think tanks, especially those that have a reputation of being right of center. In his widely read blog, University of California Professor Brad DeLong headlines a short piece on the American Enterprise Institute, "Why Oh Why Can't We Have Better Right-Wing Think Tanks?"[21] Not too surprisingly, some denizens of the think tanks hold comparably acerbic views of their university faculty counterparts—but do not publicize their differences as widely.

Criticism of the basic role of think tanks is hardly limited to their university counterparts. Some of the harshest criticism comes from think tankers themselves. For example, the late Herbert Stein, a long-term senior fellow at the American Enterprise Institute, once described think tanks as places "where like-minded people gather together to comfort each other."

The witty economist went on to note that think tank calendars are "full of conferences of people with diverse views, but the last thing that happens at such conferences is any 'conferring.'"[22] Reflecting the intellectual openness of the DC-5, these negative comments appear in a volume published by AEI!

Notes

1.   David M. Ricci, *The Transformation of American Politics: The New Washington and the Rise of Think Tanks* (New Haven: Yale University Press, 1993), p. 2.
2.   Robert L. Dilenschneider, *Power and Influence: The Rules Have Changed* (New York: McGraw-Hill, 2007).
3.   Donald E. Abelson, *A Capitol Idea: Think Tanks and U.S. Foreign Policy* (Montreal: McGill-Queen's University Press, 2006), p. 160.
4.   Author's interview with an "old Washington hand," Washington, DC, July 18, 2007.
5.   The final report of the project was published as Emile Benoit and Kenneth Boulding, eds., *Disarmament and the Economy* (New York: Harper & Row, 1963).
6.   The result was published as David Abshire and Richard Allen, eds., *National Security: Political, Military, and Economic Strategies in the Decade Ahead* (New York: Frederick Praeger, 1963).
7.   Author's interview with an experienced DC journalist, Washington, DC, July 18, 2007. He pointedly stated that he did not use the work of one of the DC-5 because of lack of trust in the integrity of their research: "They ignore evidence not supporting their conclusions."
8.   Telephone interview with experienced Washington journalist, July 2, 2007.
9.   Patrick Ford, "American Enterprise Institute for Public Policy Research," in Carol H. Weiss, ed., *Organizations for Policy Analysis* (Newbury Park, CA: Sage Publications, 1992), p. 36.
10.   Leslie R. Crutchfield and Heather McLeod Grant, *Forces for Good* (San Francisco: Jossey-Bass, 2008), p. 123.

11.   Quoted in Michael Mussa, "C. Fred Bergsten: Intellectual Entrepreneur," in Michael Mussa, editor, *C. Fred Bergsten and the World Economy* (Washington, DC: Peterson Institute for International Economics, 2006), p. 5.

12.   See, for example, Robert D. Novak, "Advising the Candidates," *International Economy*, Fall 2007, pp. 24-29.

13.   Jagdish Bhagwati, "Economic Policy in the Public Interest," *Daedalus*, Fall 2007, p. 38.

14.   Author's interview with John Hamre, president of the Center for Strategic and International Studies, Washington, DC, May 9, 2007.

15.   Dan Clawson and Mary Ann Clawson, "Reagan or Business? Foundations of the New Conservatism," in Michael Schwartz, ed., *The Structure of Power in America* (New York: Holmes & Meier, 1987), p. 205.

16.   David M. Ricci, *The Transformation of American Politics: The New Washington and the Rise of Think Tanks* (New Haven: Yale University Press, 1993), p. 164.

17.   Alice M. Rivlin, "Policy Analysis at the Brookings Institution," in Carol H. Weiss, ed., *Organizations for Policy Analysis: Helping Government Think* (Newbury Park, CA: Sage Publications, 1992), p. 26.

18.   *Ibid.*

19.   David M. Ricci, *The Transformation of American Politics: The New Washington and the Rise of Think Tanks* (New Haven: Yale University Press, 1993), p. 221.

20.   For a less benign view, see Peggy Noonan, "The GOP's 20% Problem," *Wall Street Journal*, October 13, 2007, p. W14. Noonan writes about people who leave the federal government and stay in Washington: ". . . they leave and become mosquitoes living off the pond scum, buzzing off the surface, eating well, and issuing their little stings."

21.   "Grasping Reality with Both Hands: Brad DeLong's Semi-Daily Journal," http://delong.typepad.com/, February 18, 2007, p. 19.

22.   Herbert Stein, *Presidential Economics* (Washington, DC: American Enterprise Institute, 1985), p. 325.

6

Think Tanks and Business

"Liberal academics…worry about the long-term effects on public policy because so much [think tank] scholarship is being financed by corporations and foundations."[1] That excerpt from a 1985 newspaper article on think tanks is still an accurate reflection of a widespread viewpoint among academics and many others, so it is worthy of our examination.

In my personal experience, it is the rare academic who has read the wide range of reports issued by any of the DC-5 or participated in their conferences and meetings. Rather, the negative impressions are mainly the result of reading about think tanks in what we otherwise would label dismissively as "secondary sources." Nevertheless, I take the concern seriously.

In that spirit, it is accurate to say that corporations and foundations affiliated with companies are important providers of funds for the major Washington think tanks—and for many other organizations. However, that is a very incomplete analysis of the complicated relations between business and think tanks.

As shown in Chapter 3, corporations and foundations do provide considerable financing for the major think tanks. Moreover, many foundations are affiliates of business, but some careful distinctions are necessary. The Ford Foundation, one of the largest, is quite independent of the views of the Ford family or company management. Several years ago, Henry Ford II, then-CEO of the Ford Motor Company, resigned in anger from the board of the Ford Foundation because of what he considered to be its anti-business bias. On a lesser note, I once visited the head of a foundation sponsored by a major oil company. The Foundation president made it clear that they would not even consider a proposal from an organization focusing on private enterprise, preferring to support the arts and other cultural organizations unrelated to the world of business.

As shown in Chapter 3, each of the DC-5 does receive substantial funding from corporations, private foundations, and wealthy individuals. That is a fact. Analyzing the implications is another matter and not a simple task.

It is necessary to examine the motives of business and business-oriented contributors. Then we have to analyze the ways that business can influence the decision making of their organization. Finally, we need to get an understanding of how the decision making process in the think tanks actually works and responds to the interests of major contributors.

Quite a few Washington observers believe or at least assume that think tanks are responsive to the desires of their major contributors.[2] Surely, some business support to think tanks is motivated primarily by the desire to strengthen organizations whose research and publications are viewed as supportive of the private enterprise system—and think tank managers cannot be oblivious to those concerns. AEI says that its basic purposes include "limited government, private enterprise, and a vigilant national defense." Heritage is similarly clear: "We believe in...free enterprise, limited government, a strong national defense, and traditional American values." Cato likewise is dedicated to "individual liberty, free enterprise, and a healthy skepticism of government power."

In contrast, Brookings prides itself because it "does not advance a political agenda." Similarly, CSIS focuses on providing "strategic insights and practical policy solutions to decision makers" with the emphasis on developing consensus positions on key issues of public policy.

So how can we explain that the supposedly more neutral organizations (Brookings and CSIS) proportionately garner at least as much business support as the think tanks that bluntly advertise their dedication to private enterprise? Let us see what business executives say and do on the subject.

Think Tanks as Sources of Information

The Washington representative of the Business Roundtable (the organization of 100 top corporate CEOs) states, "AEI knows what's going on...Now we understand more about the impact of ideas."[3] Clifton Garvin, former CEO of Exxon (a generous friend of think tanks), has stated, "I'm a supporter of AEI. I support others, too, like Brookings. The ability to articulate and present well-reasoned views isn't easy."[4]

A key example of Brookings' information and education activities is its Center for Executive Education. A five-day program in September 2006 covered "Inside Congress: Understanding the Legislative Process." After an initial day at Brookings, the "students" spent the rest of the time at programs on Capitol Hill where they became acquainted with key issues facing the Congress as well as some of the major players.

Somewhat less formal, the Washington Roundtable of CSIS meets three to four times a year with members of Congress, executive branch officials, and other Washington experts. Business supporters of CSIS thus have a special opportunity to be briefed on policy issues and to discuss them informally with key governmental decision-makers. An examination of the ongoing activities of any of the five major Washington-based think tanks reveals a great many efforts to raise the information level of business representatives, as well as of other influential groups in the society, on a wide range of public issues.

Robert Krieble, former CEO of Loctite Corporation, believed that "business is slowly coming to realize that the long-term success of their companies depends just as much on social policy as on management."[5] James Allen Smith confirms this point in his landmark study of think tanks:

> Briefing businessmen and consulting with firms on the global context in which they must operate has become a more important function of think tanks.[6]

On a given day, at least one of the five organizations—and several other Washington public policy institutes—will host an ambassador, a cabinet officer, or even the head of state of a foreign nation. Unlike the activities of some for-profit "hired guns," there probably will be no financial support from the country involved. Rather, the motive of the sponsoring think tank is to acquaint (or better acquaint) its audience with a particular country that is of especial interest to Americans.

Similarly, almost daily—and occasionally more frequently—a senator or prominent member of the House of Representatives will be addressing a meeting at one of the five think tanks. Likewise, some senior official of a cabinet department, White House office, or independent regulatory commission will be speaking at a session of one or more of the DC-5 (see Table 6.1 for a tabulation for one recent year). Also, each day economists or other policy specialists (such as foreign policy authorities and tax experts) will be participating at one or more public meetings of a Washington-based think tank.

To be regularly invited to such meetings—and especially to sit at a breakfast, lunch, or dinner table with one of the influential speakers—is an important opportunity for the Washington office of a large corpora-

Table 6.1
Government Officials Speaking at the DC-5 in 2005

Date	Name	Title	Topic	Think Tank
January	Rep. Mike Rogers	R-MI	Intelligence Policy	CSIS
February	Christopher Hill	Assistant Secretary of State	Korea	AEI
February	Sen. Evan Bayh	D-IN	National Security Policy	CSIS
February	Sen. Barack Obama	D-IL	Election Reform	AEI
February	Sen. Patty Murray	D-WA	Cargo Security	CSIS
February	Sen. Norman Colman	R-MN	Cargo Security	CSIS
February	Sen. Jon Kyl	R-AZ	NSA Surveillance Program	CSIS
March	Mitt Romney	Governor of Massachusetts	Education	AEI
March	Sen. Chris Dodd	D-CT	America's Infrastructure	CSIS
April	David Mulford	Ambassador to India	US-India Nuclear Cooperation	AEI
April	Sen. Gordon Smith	R-OR	Russia	CSIS

Table 6.1 (cont.)

Date	Name	Title	Topic	Think Tank
April	Rep. Bill Thomas	R-CA	Tax Policy	AEI
May	Karl Rove	White House Senior Advisor	U.S. Economy	AEI
May	Paul Wolfowitz	President, World Bank	Turkey	Brookings
May	James Connaughton	Chairman, Council of Environmental Quality	Global Warming	AEI
May	Christopher Cox	Chairman, SEC	SEC Interactive Data	AEI
May	Samuel Navarro	Vice President of Panama	Panama Canal	CSIS
May	Sen. Kay Bailey Hutchison	R-TX	Space Exploration	CSIS
May	José Miguel Insulza	Secretary General, OAS	Possible Flu Epidemic	CSIS
May	Paula Dobriansky	Undersecretary of State	Possible Flu Epidemic	CSIS
June	Michael Chertoff	Secretary, Homeland Security Dept.	Immigration and Border Control	AEI

Table 6.1 (cont.)

Date	Name	Title	Topic	Think Tank
June	Ibrahim Gambari	Undersecretary General, UN	Sudan	CSIS
June	Jendayi Frazer	Assistant Secretary of State	Sudan	CSIS
June	Edward Lazear	Chairman, Council of Economic Advisers	Tax Policy	AEI
July	Zalman Khalilzad	Ambassador	Iraq	CSIS
July	Rangin Spanta	Foreign Minister, Afghanistan	Afghanistan	CSIS
July	Sen. Russell Feingold	D-WI	HIV/AIDS	CSIS
July	Sen. Bill Frist	R-TN	HIV/AIDS	CSIS
July	Rep. Mark Kirk	R-IL	China	CSIS
July	Rep. Rich Larsen	D-WA	China	CSIS
July	Ken Nnanami	President, Nigerian Senate	Nigeria	CSIS
July	Steve Chen	Taiwan's Trade Negotiator	U.S.-Taiwan Trade	AEI
July	Kevin Warsh	Federal Reserve Governor	Liquidity	AEI

Table 6.1 (cont.)

Date	Name	Title	Topic	Think Tank
July	Mikhail Saakashvili	President of Georgia	Georgia	AEI
July	Sen. Chuck Hagel	R-NE	Middle East	Brookings
August	Mike Johannson	Secretary of Agriculture	Agricultural Policy	Cato
August	John Kufuor	President of Ghana	Foreign Aid	CSIS
August	Carlos Gutierrez	Secretary of Commerce	Cuba and Immigration Reform	Cato
September	Susan Schwab	U.S. Trade Representative	Trade Issues	CSIS
September	Neil Abercrombie	D-HI	Military Readiness	CSIS
September	Sen. Chuck Hagel	R-NE	Government-Sponsored Enterprises	AEI
September	Rep. Howard Berman	D-CA	Nuclear Proliferation	CSIS
September	Rep. Jim Leach	R-IA	Nuclear Proliferation	CSIS
September	Rep. John Spratt	D-SC	Nuclear Proliferation	CSIS
September	Stuart Levey	Undersecretary of Treasury	Terrorism and Financial Intelligence	AEI

Table 6.1 (cont.)

Date	Name	Title	Topic	Think Tank
October	Sen. Jack Reed	D-RI	Pakistan and Afghanistan	Brookings
October	Susan Schwab	U.S. Trade Representative	Trade Policy	AEI
November	Randall Kroszner	Governor, Federal Reserve	Monetary Policy	Cato
November	William Poole	President, Federal Reserve Bank of St. Louis	Monetary Policy	Cato
November	Sen. Chuck Hagel	R-NE	Public Policy	Cato

tion. At times, the event is considered so significant that invitations are obtained for the CEO or other members of the senior management.

It may appeal to the reader's sense of irony that the Council of Foreign Relations, often cited as the most prestigious think tank in the United States, is also the most direct in describing the benefits to companies who make the largest contributions. (For purposes of full disclosure, I am a long-term but not very active member of the Council.) As shown in Table 6.2, the benefits include invitations to small, private dinners with "world leaders" and annual presentations by the Council staff to the company's management. In 2006, thirty-two companies were listed as members of the President's Circle who contributed $50,000 a year or more.

Two interrelated interests are furthered by business participation in these think tank meetings. First of all, they provide an unparalleled opportunity to be "briefed" on important issues of public policy, especially those that are likely to become "hot" in the near future. There is a competitive advantage for a company to obtain a better understanding of its external environment than other firms in its industry.

It just is not practical for any individual business firm to try to duplicate the knowledge of CSIS on international affairs or of AEI on regulatory matters or of Brookings on tax issues or of Heritage on military developments or of Cato on social policy (these examples are illustrative and do not do justice to the full range of capabilities of each of the major think tanks in these and other policy areas). Some years ago, General Electric (via a division known as TEMPO) set up a broadly-based policy research division. It subsequently abandoned the effort.

As a former business planner and consultant, I know that it is hard to overestimate the importance to a company of understanding what is happening in Washington, DC. In my textbook on business and government, I identify three primary functions performed by the DC offices of American corporations: the very first is "supplying information to the home office on actions taken or contemplated by government." The second function, "Assisting in obtaining contracts," does not normally involve think tanks or their personnel. However, the third activity is quite pertinent, "Providing representation before legislative and regulatory bodies."[7]

Like the other interest groups, company officials frequently lobby or otherwise advocate that government officials take specific courses of action. An important industry has grown up in Washington consisting of lawyers, former government officials, and others who assist companies, and many other clients, in presenting their positions to government regulatory and other departments and agencies. Typically there is a formal

Table 6.2
Benefits of Corporate Membership in the President's Circle
of the Council on Foreign Relations

• Invitations to two or three small, private dinners each year with world leaders.	• Participation in more than thirty interactive conference calls with Council research fellows and other experts.
• An annual presentation on a topic related to the member company's business by a member of the Council's research staff.	• Opportunities for a select group of executives to participate in small, in-depth study groups and roundtables.
• A special invitation for a company executive to participate in at least one Council-sponsored high-level trip led by a member of the Council's leadership.	• Identification of Council research fellows as speakers for the company's board, policy committee, clients, or internal meetings.
• A special invitation to the annual dinner for the Council's Board of Directors and International Advisory Board.	• Multiple subscriptions to *Foreign Affairs*.
• The opportunity to designate two young executives as "Corporate Leaders" to participate in activities organized by the Council's Term Member Program.	• Access to the Council's exclusive Corporate website.
• Designation of a Council staff member to serve as the principal liaison to help the member company derive maximum value from its membership.	• Access to the Council's state-of-the-art reference services and library (by appointment).
• An invitation to an executive roundtable discussion with the Council's president.	• Special member rates for rental of the Harold Pratt House meeting facilities.
• Invitations to limited-seating events each year with leading figures in business and politics.	• Prominent acknowledgment in Council literature.
• Invitations for company executives to attend more than seventy events each year in New York and Washington.	

The President's Circle is the highest of the corporate membership levels.
Source: Council on Foreign Relations, 2006 *Annual Report.*

process for arranging a meeting with an executive branch official who has
authority over programs affecting business. Those formal visitations require going through a bureaucratic routine and some of the officials (e.g.,
the heads of regulatory or tax agencies) may just not be available.

Consider, under those circumstances, the opportunity facing a company
representative who is invited to a think tank meeting at which the relevant
government official is speaking. Often there is a reception prior to the
formal meeting. Thus, before the speech, there may be opportunity for
informal contacts with the speaker or an accompanying member of his
or her staff. The presentation itself may be followed by a question-and-
answer session at which the company representative may get a turn. On
the way out of the meeting, the speaker and/or accompanying members
of the staff may be available for informal conversation.[8]

It is useful to compare the think tank alternative with direct contributions by business (and other interest groups) to political decision makers.
Soon after the November 2006 elections, successful politicians in both
parties held special events in DC to raise campaign money. For example,
Representative Eric Cantor (R-VA), the new chief deputy whip for his
party in the House of Representatives, held two fundraisers. For contributions of $2,500, lobbyists had coffee with him in a private room at
Starbucks for one hour in the morning. Later that day, for donations of
$250 to $1,000, they could attend a two-hour party at a wine bar.

This is a non-partisan phenomenon in the Congress. For attendance at
a birthday party for Senator Max Baucus (D-MT), incoming chairman of
the Finance Committee, individual invitees were requested to contribute
$1,000; political action committees were expected to give $2,500. For
$5,000, a more generous donor could be a sponsor of the event.[9]

There is considerable incentive for businesses to get involved in the
development of public policy. The typical corporation is affected by a
wide array of legislative, regulatory, tax, and administrative issues. Thus,
supporting a think tank is a direct way of enhancing the opportunity for a
donor to gain knowledge of public issues and to insert the company's position into the public debate. Edward Crane, president of Cato, describes
think tanks as "highly leveraged." He is referring to the relatively modest
expenditures they incur to move an issue on to the national agenda (such
as social security privatization) and the billions of dollars involved in the
government program.[10]

There are other important reasons why companies support think tanks.
Clearly, in many cases they seek to strengthen public policy players whose
views are favorable to business in general—or to a specific industry in

the case of specialized issues. To cite some perennial examples, retail establishments are more likely to contribute to organizations publishing studies opposing general sales taxes than are manufacturing companies. Exporters are far more interested in supporting advocates of free trade than industries adversely affected by foreign competition. Businesses that have become accustomed to detailed regulation are not exactly antagonistic to extending regulation to other firms. Those other companies are more likely to provide funds for a think tank whose research shows the benefits of reduced regulation.

A little later in this chapter I will examine more deeply the ways in which businesses try to influence the position of a think tank. At this point, let us continue to identify the different ways in which a company benefits from involvement with a major think tank. Each of the major think tanks has in residence people who are considered influential in the intellectual and public life of the nation. These luminaries range from former cabinet officers and Federal Reserve board members to retired senators and representatives to retired generals and admirals and former ambassadors as well as distinguished and well-known academics. I have seen first hand and on numerous occasions the CEO of a major corporation being charmed by one of these outstanding personalities.

Being listed as a generous supporter of a mainstream think tank (such as the Brookings Institution) may also enhance the institutional image of a firm. I suggest that the cumulative effect of a think tank relationship, as briefly described here, may justify a generous contribution by the most hard-nosed business decision maker.

Impact of Business on Think Tank Positions

Let us now turn to perhaps the most controversial aspect of the relationships between business and think tanks: the worry that those who provide the financial support for a think tank are in a position to influence the positions taken by its researchers on public issues. I must confess that this concern about the impact of financing on research has worried me over a long professional career that includes serving as a business executive, a "high ranking" government official, and a professor who seeks outside financial support for summer research and expensive projects during the academic year.

I cannot quickly dismiss the concern that "he who pays the piper calls the tune." Unfortunately, there is strong evidence of such situations in universities as well as in government and in business.[11] Under the circumstances, I am not surprised that think tanks are not immune from such pressures. That does not justify the pressures that a think tank may feel from its financial supporters, but I believe that the context is worthy of some attention.

At the bureaucratic or operational level, when a university—or a think tank—accepts grants or contracts from the federal government, it has to agree to abide by the government's rules for keeping its books and restricting its outlays to categories specified by the government. Like defense contractors, universities quickly learn that costs incurred to carry out a federal contract that are not "allowed" by the governmental auditor must come out of the institution's own financial reserves. I am not aware of any company that imposes similar detailed restrictions on its grants to think tanks or universities.

Some of the impacts of government on universities are even more obtrusive and in a fundamental way. For example, several friends of mine teaching at a major state university (but without tenure) reported that their appointments were terminated when their public positions on subsidizing local industries ran counter to the position of powerful political interests. Likewise, William Niskanen was apparently fired as chief economist of the Ford Motor Company for consistently taking in public a free trade position at a time when the automobile industry was advocating barriers to automobile imports. (He is now chairman of the Cato Institute.) Similarly, political appointees without the protection of a civil service appointment are easily terminated when they depart from the party line.

In government, it is not unusual for a federal agency or congressional committee providing funding to private researchers (such as think tanks) to require its approval—or at least review—before the publication of the results. In my experience, companies are much more likely to provide "no strings attached" general support to a university research center (or to a think tank) than is a government agency. On reflection, this statement of what I believe is the reality runs counter to the prevailing opinion in academia.

Moreover, the impact of business support on universities is real, although not necessarily insidious. Derek Bok, the retired president of Harvard University, believes that wealthy donors can clearly alter the shape of the institution. He cites the "opulence" of business schools with the "shabbiness" of schools of education.[12]

What about think tanks? As noted in earlier chapters, the selection of research personnel is the key way in which the organization imposes its general philosophy on its employees. Unlike a learned journal where the referees reviewing a submitted manuscript do not know the identity of the author, a think tank hiring a senior researcher is faced with a substantial track record. As a result, a certain organizational spirit pervades the "tank" and influences its attractiveness to potential new hires.

In the case of Heritage, for example, the long-term leader, as quoted earlier, states clearly that "Everyone at Heritage works from a common policy perspective."[13] Brookings, in contrast, holds a very different official position, focusing on analysis of issues. In practice, however, the output of a Brookings scholar is often as predictably "moderate" or left of center as the Heritage researchers are "conservative" or right of center. (I may have just insulted friends at Brookings who, on occasion, have asked me to review a manuscript or speak at a meeting.) I must add that in my view—and that of many others—the level of scholarship at Brookings is very much higher than for think tanks in general. Nevertheless, to any experienced observer in the nation's capital, there is a clear product differentiation among think tanks in terms of policy orientation.

Under the circumstances, it is neither necessary nor effective for a business interest to attempt to pressure one of the major think tanks to support its position on a given issue. First of all, the interest group can choose from a variety of think tanks and for-profit organizations each possessing a somewhat different position in the policy spectrum. In selecting which think tanks to support, the savvy business executive does not expect to find 100 percent agreement between the positions of a given think tank and the desires of an individual company. When I ran a university-based think tank (the Center for the Study of American Business), this became clear on many occasions at meetings with existing and prospective contributors. More recently, the Heritage Foundation stated that it strongly opposed the Medicare drug entitlement in 2003 despite the support of the bill by many of its major donors.[14]

Business firms also have alternatives to think tanks in terms of players in the public policy arena. Companies facing strong competition from imports (especially the smaller and less diversified firms) can call on the U.S. Business & Industry Council for sympathetic research. Likewise, unions concerned about the loss of domestic jobs to foreign firms support think tanks such as the Economic Policy Institute. In both cases, the interest groups know that the researchers at the five major think tanks will not take a protectionist viewpoint on international trade issues.

Secondly, the leadership of any of the DC-5 will as a matter of policy deflect overt pressure to take a specific position on controversial issues.

Many individual researchers at these think tanks will bridle at the effort of any outsider to influence their analyses. That hands-off position is justified on two closely-related bases. To begin with, the experienced think tank leader knows that the influence and effectiveness of the institution's work depends in large measure on the respect for their output by the government and media users. The researchers and analysts who are the key assets of these organizations are typically professionals who will initially resent and ignore the pressure and ultimately resign from the organization to maintain their professional independence.

Each of the major think tanks devotes a substantial amount of resources to fundraising from a diverse array of contributors. That diversity of funding sources is fundamental to success. With dozens if not hundreds of firms and foundations providing support—plus in some cases thousands of smaller contributors—a think tank can afford to take independent positions on controversial public issues. Without pushing the point too far, there is a parallel here with the case of contributors to political campaigns. There is a considerable body of serious research on the topic that demonstrates that contributors typically support the politicians who already have taken the positions they favor, rather than trying to get them to change their views.

As Representative Barney Frank (D-MA) has stated, "I don't think that votes follow money. I think that money follows votes."[15] Empirical research confirms that point. A study at Bard College demonstrates that campaign money tends to flow to candidates who support the group's position rather than the group trying to influence the candidate to change a policy position already taken.[16] I believe that this evidence is far more relevant than the dramatic examples of congressional bribery à la Jack Abramoff. The later type of actions do not relate to the broad public policy concerns on which think tanks are focused.

The subject of business support of think tanks is one on which even the most sensible academics can take positions that can only be described as silly. For example, professor Andrew Rich has lamented that his research on think tanks showed that "Wealthy conservative supporters were generally not available to non-conservative organizations."[17] He could have said with equal accuracy that wealthy non-conservative supporters were not generally available to conservative organizations. Among many others, multimillionaire George Soros is well known as a generous supporter of, to put it mildly, "non-conservative" organizations.

The Spectrum of Relationships

The relationship between a nonprofit think tank and its funding sources is both complex and subtle. We can think of a spectrum extending from simple support (similar to donations to a symphony orchestra) to the think tank serving almost as an outsourcing venture for the donor's business interests.

At one end of this spectrum, we find some foundations and private companies that provide general support, "no strings attached" funding. The subtlety in this case involves the fact that an established think tank has a track record of reports and statements on a variety of controversial public policies as well as a basic cadre of researchers who have taken positions on specific issues. Thus, even the granting of nominally "no strings attached" financing can be based on reasonable but implicit assumptions as to the purposes to which the funds will be devoted. Brookings will not be issuing a handbook on Marxism in the foreseeable future nor will AEI be publishing a report showing the advantages of deregulating "hard" drugs.

At the other end of the spectrum is the "job shop" operation. Here the organization providing the money is quite specific as to the ultimate product that it expects to receive. In many cases, an array of non-profit and for-profit research organizations will compete for a given contract or grant to be awarded. Especially in the case of government agencies, the funding source imposes specific requirements that may include its prior approval before the research organization can publicly report on the work.

In many cases, the relationship between the funding source and the research organization takes a position toward the middle of the spectrum. For example, the financial supporter of a think tank may specify the general area of research that it will contribute to. An example might be reforming the tax structure to promote economic growth or developing a strategy for the United States in dealing with a specific foreign country (e.g., China or Iran). But, in the first case, the think tank will not pledge in advance that the study will support a flat tax nor, in the second case, that its report will advocate a program of direct foreign aid.

The "no strings attached" approach most likely is the one that the public would normally expect in the case of tax-exempt think tanks, contributions to which are deductible in computing federal income tax liability. In striking contrast, the polar alternative of a "job shop" possesses elements of unfair competition with tax paying firms. But, far more important, responding very specifically to the needs of a sponsor (or, to use the business term, client) raises serious questions as to the intellectual independence of the think tank.

These issues involve lots of judgment calls and underscore the critical factor of confidence in the integrity of the think tank leadership. As a practical matter, the larger the portion of current expenses that is covered by earnings from the organization's endowment, the easier it is for the think tank to exercise its independent judgment. Somewhat similarly, the greater the proportion of current revenues that is obtained from a large variety of providers of general support, the easier it is to maintain the intellectual independence of the research organization.

Some flavor of the subtleties involved in the relationship between business and think tanks is conveyed in an interview that a political scientist held with Bruce MacLaury, then president of Brookings, on the subject of raising money from business:

> . . . you have to justify that you are doing not only credible work but relevant and visible work, and that you are not just perceived as being knee-jerk liberal.[18]

Think Tank Boards of Directors

One avenue for business influence on think tanks is to serve on their governing boards (boards of directors or trustees). As someone who has served on the governing boards of a variety of business and non-profit organizations, I am aware of the powers—and limits—of board membership. A few generalizations from personal experience may provide a useful starting point.

At one extreme is the successful organization, be it for-profit or otherwise, that is in a strong financial condition and meeting or outperforming its program objectives. At the other extreme is the organization that is facing deep financial difficulties and perhaps also not performing well on substantive grounds. In the first case, the board is likely to govern with a light touch, granting the top management very substantial flexibility and discretion in its decision making. In the second case, the board almost always assumes an extremely activist position (like an imminent hanging, the threat of bankruptcy is guaranteed to arouse the most somnolent board member).

However, most of the time and especially for the five think tanks covered in this report, the governance by the board is somewhere in between the two extremes. Like non-profit organizations generally, an outside director serves as the board chairman but more than a few other members accept their position for its honorific value or because they are substantial contributors. The size of the boards of the "DC-5" ranges from forty-four in the case of Brookings to fourteen for Cato. The average of twenty-seven members is more than double the average of eleven for a Fortune 1000 company, but comparable to or lower than many other non-profit institutions such as universities, hospitals, and museums. Therefore, in practice—and especially for the larger boards—the chairs of the key committees and usually a hard core of other seriously committed members assume the bulk of the task of governance as well as leadership in fundraising.

As in the case of business boards, the full-time CEO is acknowledged as the leader of the organization. Indeed, board members in general desire a situation where the CEO inspires their confidence and they can accept his or her recommendations on most matters. Rarely do the directors even try to get involved in selecting specific staff members or research projects. In the case of think tanks, often some portion of the board meeting is devoted, not to governance matters, but to briefing the members on interesting new research being performed by the staff or giving them an analysis of current policy issues by some of the think tank's "stars." Indeed, those briefings are part of the benefits of serving as an unpaid director of a major think tank.

In any event, there is opportunity at think tank board meetings for individual members to raise issues of governance, be they related to staffing or to substantive programs. But, on balance, given the diversity of the composition of board membership, I find it difficult to join the critics who tend to automatically associate business membership on a think tank board with business control of its policy agenda.

In recent years, only one of the five DC-based think tanks experienced a period of serious financial crisis. In that case, when William Baroody, senior, retired from the presidency of AEI, the board appointed his son as successor. For a variety of reasons, that turned out to be an error of judgment. AEI began a period of especially rapid expansion both in size and in the scope of its programs. Although at first revenues continued growing, they could not keep up with the need to balance outgo with income.

The board did step in, replacing the top management while several board members provided the funds, which in effect prevented bankruptcy. In the process, AEI returned to its earlier position of relatively right of center in public policy matters (from a temporarily very diffused approach to public policy issues). Strong new management once again inspired the confidence of the board and of funding sources, demonstrating the organization's continuing ability to command the respect of the various "publics" it serves.

Michael Walker, senior fellow at Canada's Fraser Institute, has provided some useful guidelines for boards of think tanks. Those guidelines are cited here because they are consistent with my own experiences!

1. The board must be active enough to provide advice and guidance based on business experience but not so active as to interfere with the independence of the researchers and the research agenda of the organization.
2. The successful think tank must be independent of its sources of financing.
3. Ideally, the board should only be involved in an oversight function regarding the financial affairs of the institute and not involved in setting the research agenda.[19]

Conclusion

As we have seen, a major force for maintaining the independence and quality of the think tanks in general and the five major DC-based think tanks in particular is the continuing strong competition each of them feels. That competition comes from the other four as well as from the many other sources of public policy research and analysis that are available to the Congress, the media, and the public generally. Surely, none of the DC-5 enjoys a monopoly position in the Washington public policy community!

Notes

1. Peter H. Stone, "Not-So-Strange Bedfellows in Conservative Think Tanks," *Washington Post National Weekly*, June 17, 1985, p. 12.
2. Telephone interview with an experienced Washington journalist, July 2, 2007.
3. Sidney Blumenthal, *The Rise of the Counter-Establishment* (New York: Times Books, 1986), p. 42.
4. *Ibid.*, p. 53.
5. Quoted in Peter H. Stone, "Not-So-Strange Bedfellows in Conservative Think Tanks," *Washington Post National Weekly*, June 17, 1985, p. 11.
6. James Allen Smith, *The Idea Brokers* (New York: Free Press, 1991), p. 210.
7. Murray L. Weidenbaum, *Business and Government in the Global Marketplace*, Seventh Edition (Upper Saddle River, NJ: Pearson Prentice Hall, 2004), p. 299.
8. "Essential to all think tanks are events at which donors rub shoulders with Washington personages," Gregg Easterbrook, "Ideas Move Nations," *Atlantic Monthly*, February 1986, p. 5.
9. Robert Pear, "Time to Party in the Capital. Just Bring the Checkbook," *New York Times*, December 8, 2006, p. A26.
10. Author's interview with Edward Crane, President of the Cato Institute, Washington, DC, June 19, 2007.

11. Some academics devote substantial amounts of time and effort to testifying in antitrust and other law cases on behalf of specific business clients. See George Anders, "An Economist's Courtroom Bonanza," *The Wall Street Journal*, March 19, 2007, p. A-1 et ff.

12. Derek Bok, *Universities in the Marketplace* (Princeton: Princeton University Press, 2003), p. 6.

13. Edwin Feulner, "The Heritage Foundation," in James G. McGann and R. Kent Weaver, editors, *Think Tanks and Civil Societies* (New Brunswick, NJ: Transaction Publishers, 2000), p. 73.

14. "Think Tanks Talk Back," *Washington Post*, August 8, 2007, p. A15.

15. Quoted in Catherine Morrison, *Managing Corporate Political Action Committees* (New York: Conference Board, 1986), pp. v-vi.

16. Christopher Magee, *Campaign Contributions, Policy Decisions, and Election Outcomes* (New York: Levy Economic Institute of Bard College, 2001).

17. See Andrew Rich, *Think Tanks, Public Policy, and the Politics of Expertise* (Cambridge: Cambridge University Press, 2004), p. 65.

18. Quoted in David M. Ricci, *The Transformation of American Politics* (New Haven:. Yale University Press, 1993), p. 69.

19. Michael Walker, "Some Lessons from the Engine Room About Managing An Institute," *Atlas Highlights*, Winter 2006/07, p. 11.

7

Measuring the Influence of Think Tanks

It is difficult, and often inaccurate, to present great conclusions about the role and influence of the major think tanks. Surely their influence varies by organization, issue, and time period. At times, Brookings and Heritage attract much attention for the views of their researchers on tax reform while the analyses of scholars from AEI, Cato, and CSIS on other economic issues or foreign policy are widely covered. On other occasions, the positions of different organizations are given more weight. These other groups range from smaller think tanks to large trade associations to law firms to college faculty. Sometimes, none of these private sector organizations get much attention. The focus may be on the views of the key members of the executive and legislative branches.

On broad issues of trade policy, for example, the opinion of the large think tanks and also the relevant smaller ones are widely solicited. On narrower matters relating to protecting individual products and industries, the representatives of specific interest groups (telecommunications, oil, utilities, retailing, banking, labor unions, etc.) are considered to be much more relevant and their positions may be given considerable weight. All this demonstrates the obvious point that the major think tanks are neither invariably key contributors to all public policy issues nor are they devoid of influence.

Of course, there is an inevitable amount of puffery in the claims of individual think tanks, especially when they are raising money or reporting to their supporters. Many difficulties arise in evaluating the results of their activities. An example is the case of nationally known figures (such as former cabinet members and legislative leaders) who have only a part-time affiliation with a think tank. It is a great temptation for the think tank to claim credit for all of the widely covered public policy statements and activities of these highly visible individuals. Yet none of that gets to the heart of the matter: the actual impact of think tanks on government action.

Measuring the Impact

A fundamental and frustrating question faces analysts of the think tank phenomenon as well as the leaders and supporters of these organizations: how can we measure their effectiveness in the public policy arena? There are readily available and useful measures of inputs, notably the resources used. (Financial data for the DC-5 were presented in Chapters 2 and 3.) Measures of output—the accomplishments in terms of actual changes in public policy that have been achieved—are far more relevant. As we will see later in this chapter, however, such output measures are also much more illusive and difficult to develop.

Nevertheless, useful knowledge about the operations of think tanks may be gained by examining available measures of the "intermediate" products of think tanks. The substantial amount of resources available to the DC-5 gives each of them the opportunity to attract expert researchers and to devote considerable time and effort to analyzing important issues of public policy (see Table 7.1 for the broad range of issues that they cover). In addition, each of the DC-5 invests substantially in ways to disseminate widely the results of their research and analysis. A key part of their "public" consists of decision makers in the legislative and executive branches of the national government. As one academic analyst of think tanks has written, these organizations are relatively cost-effective compared to universities and other research organizations. "Dollar for dollar, think tanks attract greater attention than most any other organizational source of expertise."[1]

Each of the DC-5, and many other think tanks, are pleased to report the number of publications they issue, the frequency that their staff members appear on national television, and the numerous citations of their activity in the print media. These are all useful indicators of their efforts to influence public policy and should not be ignored. As economists measure output, however, these are at best "intermediate goods," comparable to the engineering and marketing that goes into the production and sale of an automobile. The final output is properly measured in terms comparable to the number and value (or price) of the vehicles actually produced in a given time period. That topic is covered a little later in this chapter.

The widely-used indicators of intermediate "output" also require some interpretation. For example, reporting the number of books written by a group's scholars does not distinguish between those widely distributed

Table 7.1
Major Program Areas of Think Tanks

AEI	BROOKINGS	CATO	CSIS	HERITAGE
Economic Policy	Foreign Policy	Constitutional Studies	New Drivers of Global	Budget and Taxation
General Economics	Cooperative Security	Educational Freedom	Security	Commerce and Infrastructure
International Trade and	Global Sustainability	Representative Government	Biotechnology	Crime, Justice, and the Law
Finance	Conflict Resolution	Trade Policy	Energy	Economic and Political
Environmental Policy	International	Defense and Foreign Policy	Global Aging	Thought
Regulation	Development	Fiscal Policy	Global Strategy	Education
Health Policy		Health and Welfare	Governance	Family, Culture, and
	Economic Studies	National Resources	HIV/AIDS	Community
Foreign and Defense Policy	Productivity	Global Economic Liberty	International Trade	Federalism, Governing, and
United States	Trade		Islam	Elections
Latin America	Deregulation		Technology	First Principles
Middle East	Education			Foreign Policy
Developing World	Poverty		Defense and Security	Health and Welfare
Asia	Welfare		International Security	Information Technology
	Energy		Post-Conflict Recon-	Labor
Social and Political Studies	Telecommunications		struction	National Security
Political			Defense Industry	Natural Resources and
Social and Cultural	Metropolitan Policy		Homeland Security	Environment
Education			Regional Security	Regulation and Deregulation
Legal and Constitutional			Transnational Threats	
			Regional Programs	
			Africa	
			Americas	
			Asia	
			Europe	

Source: Reports from think tanks.

volumes that have a national impact and the more specialized works that appeal to a more limited scholarly or technical audience. Citations in the *Congressional Record* and in congressional hearings and committee reports may be more indicative of policy impact than the sheer number of materials published and distributed. Yet at times a case may be made that the most common form of use of expertise by public policy decision makers is quite perfunctory—to support a preexisting position.[2]

Meetings held constitute an especial heterogeneous category of activities. Some conferences attract large numbers of journalists and congressional staff and others have very modest rosters of attendees. A few meetings surface important new ideas by think tank researchers and many others merely provide a platform for the repetition of well-known positions of government officials and interest group representatives.

Data on still other think tank activities are even more difficult to judge. A lecture by a staff member to a university audience may demonstrate the intellectual power of a think tank or merely confirm the faculty's negative view of the researchers who work in think tanks. A speech to a campus-wide audience may have a very different impact than a presentation to a graduate seminar.

Likewise, media exposure of think tank staff members ranges from brief appearances on a local television station to a long and featured interview on a national network, and from a guest editorial ("op-ed") in a widely read newspaper to a brief mention in a long article in a magazine of limited circulation.

One study of the four-year period January 2001-January 2005 showed that the DC-5 dominated media coverage of foreign affairs and military issues compared to the more specialized think tanks, such as the Council on Foreign Relations, the Hudson Institute, the Hoover Institution, the Carnegie Endowment for International Peace, and RAND. The DC-5 accounted for 57 percent of the think tank coverage in six major newspapers and 51 percent of the exposure on the national TV networks.[3]

Substantial variations occurred for individual think tanks. Brookings dominated the television coverage with 40 percent of the total, with Heritage in second place amongst the DC-5. In the case of the print media, Brookings' more modest first-place share of 19 percent was followed fairly closely by CSIS with 14 percent. In congressional testimony on foreign and military issues during the same four-year period, the major players were CSIS (with a 28 percent share), Brookings with 18 percent, and AEI with 12 percent.[4]

Yet another comparison is provided in a study published in the No-vember 2005 issue of the *Quarterly Journal of Economics*. It analyzed the use by members of Congress of the works of Washington think tanks during the years 1993-2002.[5] On a scale of 100 representing citations only by Democrats and zero exclusively by Republicans, 50.0 registered perfect neutrality. Brookings and CSIS came closest to the center, 53.3 for Brookings (slightly more Democratic usage) and CSIS at 46.3 (slightly preferred by Republicans). The other three members of the DC-5 were shown to generate far greater citations by Republicans than Democrats (36.6 for AEI, 36.3 for Cato, and 20.0 in the case of Heritage).

At this point, let us turn to measures of think tank outputs. After all, their end product is not the visibility achieved by these organizations but their impact in terms of improvements in public policy.

Measuring Output

As many previous studies of the American think tank phenomenon have demonstrated, the major Washington think tanks have earned an important presence in the Washington policy community. Actually trying to measure their impact on specific public policy changes, however, has frustrated scholars for years. Their general conclusion is reminiscent of the judge who did not define pornography precisely, but said in effect, "I know it when I see it" (the direct comparison with think tanks is surely unwarranted). Nevertheless, political scientist David Ricci summed up the state-of-knowledge on the subject quite accurately: "Power in Washington cannot be measured precisely, yet think tanks surely have a good deal of it . . ."[6]

There are many reasons why analysts of the think tank phenomenon (including me) cannot be more precise in attempting to measure the output of these organizations. A basic obstacle is the extended nature of the public policy process. As noted in Chapter 1, it typically takes many years for an idea to be transformed into a specific public policy decision. Christopher DeMuth, AEI's president, estimated that, even for success-ful ventures, it often took at least twelve years from the time a public policy proposal was made to its enactment.[7] In the process, a variety of individuals and organizations, in government as well as the private sec-tor, are involved in the inevitable modification of the original idea into a specific statute or regulation.

Take the case of the general tax reductions enacted by Congress in 2001. AEI tells us that two of their scholars (Lawrence Lindsey and Glenn Hubbard, who held the senior economic positions in the Bush

White House at the time) were instrumental in developing and successfully promoting the basic ideas.[8] Simultaneously, a scholar at Brookings (Isabel Sawhill) is given the credit for developing the specific provision (a liberalization of the child tax credit), which was key to getting the critical support of several fence-sitting New England Republicans.[9] Sawhill, however, has described her role as that of an analyst, leaving the advocacy to others, notably Robert Greenstein of the Center on Budget and Policy Priorities.[10] Also, Heritage conducted ambitious and persistent efforts to develop public and legislative support for the tax cuts. Its tax experts were cited repeatedly in the floor debate on the tax bill.

To this observer, each of the think tanks that claimed a role in the 2001 tax cuts is basically correct. Yet the list of key players in that drama extends to the leaders of the House Ways and Means Committee and the Senate Finance Committee as well as Karl Rove, the White House's most senior political adviser. Perhaps most fundamentally, President George W. Bush laid out the basic tax program in his 2000 campaign to be elected president.

John Hamre, leader of CSIS, provides the cynical conclusion of a veteran Washingtonian: evaluating the role of a given think tank in affecting an important change in public policy reminds him of the case of Anna Nicole Smith's baby, where several men volunteered that they were the father. However, in the case of public policy there is no equivalent of a DNA test to declare the parentage with a comparable degree of certainty![11]

Two serious scholars of the subject conclude, "Determining the extent to which a think tank or group of think tanks influenced a particular policy decision remains a daunting methodological task."[12] One senior think tank political scientist states that how to measure the impact of a think tank is the subject of constant internal discussions. He notes that, because of the elusive nature of "impact" and the multiplicity of players, all of the think tanks fall back on indirect measures, notably the creation of bodies of research and proposals that have helped to shape public policy.[13] Perhaps Edwin Feulner, the president of the Heritage Foundation, has presented the most straightforward response to the question of measuring the impact of think tanks, ". . . we still have no clear answers."[14] An even more pessimistic conclusion was reached by David Frum of AEI, a former White House speech writer. When asked what indicators are useful in evaluating the influence of think tanks, he replied, "None. You can't measure influence."[15]

Nevertheless, an upbeat assessment of the Washington think tank phenomenon was provided by the *National Journal* in a report on the activities of Brookings and AEI. After agreeing that measuring their relative impact is "an elusive task at best," the reporter ended on a more positive note: perhaps their more important function is providing experienced professionals whose analysis and commentary on the day-to-day developments are available to the various participants in the public policy process.[16]

Surely, each of the five think tanks analyzed here are important sources of information to the media, the government, and to a host of private interest groups, all of whom are involved in the public policy process. Their staff analysts usually understand the world of policymakers. They have observed it closely and quite a few of them have directly participated in it.

One knowledgeable analyst of think tanks has observed that Washington think tanks have grown because their sponsors believed that people in the city would pay more attention to their policy advice than to the views of lobbyists or other special pleaders. That, on reflection, is a powerful albeit unmeasurable conclusion for a city where the same author notes, quite correctly, "…tens of thousands of …policy-minded people spend most of their working time trying to influence the course of government decisions."[17] Nevertheless, in the following section I try to show the importance—and limitations—of think tanks during one particularly active period of Washington policymaking.

A Case Study of Think Tanks and One Presidential Administration

It is easy to overestimate, or to underestimate, the ability of think tanks, especially the major Washington-based ones, to influence the policy decisions of government. This section examines the role of think tanks in developing the programs and policies of one presidency. The opening year of the Administration of President Ronald Reagan provides an opportunity to demonstrate both the impacts and the limitations of think tanks in the public policy process.

During 1980 the Reagan campaign established numerous task forces to deal with the issues that Governor Reagan would face if he became president. These task forces covered economic areas—inflation, taxes, etc.—as well as many other subjects, ranging from national defense to strategic minerals. In the case of economic issues, an umbrella group was set up under the chairman of former Secretary of the Treasury George Shultz (a professional economist who earlier had served as dean of the Graduate School of Business at the University of Chicago).[18] At the same time, many Republican activists and others were sending the Reagan campaign headquarters all sorts of proposals and advice.

Early in 1981, the Reagan Administration presented and vigorously pursued four key "pillars" of the Reagan economic program (often called "Reaganomics"). These four were cutting government spending, reducing taxes, reforming regulation, and promoting a strong monetary policy to bring down inflation.[19] Let us examine the intellectual background of each of these four "pillars." I start with regulatory reform because the role of think tanks was most direct.

Regulatory Reform

Two of the major Washington think tanks were especially active in developing the ideas for reforming the complex system of government regulation of the private sector. Here the work of think tanks and university researchers was closely related and clearly effective. There were many contributors to the cumulative effort over an extended period of time.

An influential study by John R. Meyer of Harvard and his associates was published in 1959 by the Harvard University Press. *The Economics of Competition in the Transportation Industries*[20] gave the initial impetus for a series of more specialized analyses. In 1972, AEI sponsored and published *Freight Transportation Regulation*,[21] written by Thomas Gale Moore of the Hoover Institution of Stanford University. In 1974, George Douglas of the University of North Carolina and James C. Miller III, then at Texas A&M University, wrote *Economic Regulation of Domestic Air Transport*.[22] That book was sponsored and published by Brookings.

AEI sponsored and published in the 1970s a series of studies on the shortcomings of government regulation: Sam Peltzman (of the University of Chicago) on pharmaceutical regulation, John Gould (also of the University of Chicago) on the Davis-Bacon Act, and Rita Ricardo Campbell (of Stanford's Hoover Institution) on food safety regulation.[23] AEI also published my wide-ranging report on the high cost of government regulation,[24] which attracted an unusual amount of attention in the media and subsequently in business and government circles.

In September 1980, candidate Reagan appointed a task force on regulatory reform to prepare recommendations for his administration should he be elected. The task force consisted of university and think tank economists most of whom were active in the field of regulation, including three of the authors mentioned above (James C. Miller III, Thomas Gale Moore, and I, who served as chairman).

The task force recommended several reforms, which drew on the work that had been done by economic and legal scholars over the previous two decades. Our recommendations included: (1) requiring federal agencies to perform benefit-cost analyses to justify new regulations; (2) appointing regulators who were concerned both with attaining the objectives of regulation and minimizing the burdens imposed; (3) establishing a new White House office to monitor new regulations; and (4) setting a temporary moratorium on new regulations to provide a breather to review the performance of the existing regulatory system.[25] These proposals were adopted in early 1981 and enabled the new Administration to get off to a speedy start on reforming regulation. Several members of the task force were appointed to strategic positions in the regulatory policy area, most notably, James Miller as executive director of the President's Task Force on Regulatory Relief. (As chairman of the Council of Economic Advisers, I served as a member of the Task Force.)

Reducing Government Spending

Cutting back on the growth of federal spending is part and parcel of traditional Republican doctrine. It certainly was a fundamental part of candidate Ronald Reagan's thinking about government. Thus, in the planning for the incoming Reagan Administration, there never was any serious debate about the desirability of cutting the federal budget. Rather, attention was focused on which program areas to cut and how much.

Over the years, a wide variety of organizations had prepared critiques of government programs and expenditures[26] and the results reinforced the strong attitude toward economy in government. A Reagan transition task force on the federal budget was chaired by former Nixon cabinet officer James T. Lynn. The need for budget cutting was reinforced by a widely-circulated memo by Congressman David Stockman (R-MI) who warned in November 1980 of an economic Dunkirk unless strong actions were taken.[27] Stockman subsequently was appointed the first budget director in the Reagan Administration. Many of the specific budget reductions were proposed by the President's Budget Working Group, chaired by Stockman (the other two members were Martin Anderson, on leave from Stanford University's Hoover Institution and the author, on leave from Washington University).

However, simultaneously a different set of plans was being developed—to respond to the widespread desire to strengthen the U.S. military establishment after years of budgetary restraint.[28] Often the same people, especially Ronald Reagan, shared both viewpoints—that government spending should be slowed down while military outlays should be accelerated. The process of reconciling these two different views on the future of the federal budget turned out to be a substantial challenge to the incoming administration. Although many think tanks, university research groups, and other interested organizations issued reports on one or another of the two different approaches, I do not recall any extended effort to reconcile them.

Nevertheless, the single most influential policy report available to the public at that time was Heritage's *Mandate for Leadership*.[29] That report hit a responsive chord with the media and the Congress in presenting, in simple language, a comprehensive array of proposals for helping to achieve President Reagan's program objectives.

The initial Reagan budgets combined substantial expansions in military outlays with proposals to cut back or slow down the growth of numerous civilian spending programs. Concurrent tax cuts and a tight monetary policy—reducing the level of economic activity—combined to slow down the growth of federal revenues, especially in the short run. The result was unprecedented huge budget deficits.

Cutting Taxes

Reducing tax burdens was basic to conservative thinking in the years leading up to the Reagan presidency and a key part of his 1980 presidential campaign. As someone who faced extremely high marginal rates in his Hollywood days, Ronald Reagan did not need any prompting on that score. Thus, no special effort was made to draw on the formal scholarly literature on the impact of taxation on economic incentives.

Three specific reinforcing factors deserve to be mentioned. First of all, economist Arthur Laffer (at the time at the University of Southern California) had developed the notion of the Laffer curve as a way of showing visually the revenue effects of reducing high marginal tax rates (and the conditions under which tax revenues would rise with rate reductions). Although the official statements of the Reagan Administration on tax policy did not adopt Laffer's analysis, his public involvement in the debate on the topic enhanced the movement for reducing federal tax rates.

The second factor had a direct impact on the Reagan tax policy. The Kemp-Roth tax proposals (introduced by Congressman Jack Kemp (R-NY) and Senator William Roth (R-DE)) focused on across-the-board reductions of the high marginal tax rates—the top rate on the personal income tax was then 70 percent! This was the center-piece of a supply-side economic strategy.[30] The intellectual contribution to that strategy of Columbia University economist Robert Mundell was important, especially in the effort to reconcile stimulating tax cuts with inflation-curbing monetary restraint.

The third element in developing the Reagan tax program was the Carleton Group, so-named because its meetings took place in the Sheraton-Carleton Hotel in Washington, DC. This informal array of Washington tax lawyers, lobbyists, and business representatives met weekly during 1980-81 to develop and advance an agenda for tax reform. It focused on the investment incentives, specifically accelerated depreciation, which became a basic part of the Reagan tax program. The group also promoted the multiyear reductions in personal income tax rates advanced by Congressman Jack Kemp, who was a member of the Carleton Group.[31]

In September 1980, candidate Ronald Reagan appointed a task force of tax experts to develop specific proposals (including at least one member of the Carleton Group, tax attorney Ernest Christian). Chaired by Charls Walker, a former Deputy Secretary of the Treasury, the group proposed a combination of tax rate reductions à la Kemp-Roth and investment incentives to business developed by the Carleton Group. In office, the Reagan Administration carried out these reforms by successfully proposing to the Congress three annual installments of across-the-board cuts in the personal income tax plus more generous depreciation allowances to stimulate business investment.[32]

Monetary Policy

In the case of monetary policy, Milton Friedman had the fundamental impact on Ronald Reagan's thinking in 1981-82 (I witnessed it while serving as chairman of President Reagan's Council of Economic Advisers). Friedman was the dominating presence in the discussions of monetary policy. This was true both in face-to-face interactions with the President, notably at the meetings of the President's Economic Policy Advisory Board, as well as via some of the senior economists of the monetarist school who were serving at the Treasury and the CEA. Indeed, the Reagan Administration relied primarily on monetary restraint on the part of the Federal Reserve to bring down the inflation the nation faced in 1981-82.

At an operational level, the dominant figure in the conduct of U.S. monetary policy during that period was Paul Volcker, the chairman of the Federal Reserve System. Although initially appointed by President Jimmy Carter, Volcker embarked on an ambitious effort to shift the focus of monetary policy from a preoccupation with interest rates to include broader consideration of the monetary aggregates, notably the money supply.

Friedman was not alone in developing the support in the economics profession for the "monetarist" approach to macroeconomics. Important contributions were made by Karl Brunner of the University of Rochester, Alan Meltzer of Carnegie Mellon University, the economic staff of the Federal Reserve Bank of St. Louis, and many others.

Within the economics profession, it is generally recognized that Friedman's fundamental contribution to the monetary literature was the book he co-authored with Anna Schwartz, *A Monetary History of the United States.*[33] That study was sponsored by the National Bureau of Economic Research (then headquartered in New York and now in Massachusetts). Friedman was a long-time research associate of the National Bureau and Schwartz was a long-time employee of the organization.

Friedman, at the time of writing the book and for many years thereafter, was a chaired professor of economics at the University of Chicago. During the years that followed the publication of *Monetary History*, a generation of economists developed and promoted the monetarist viewpoint, which emphasized the role of the money supply in influencing the course of inflation in an economy.

Reaganomics and Think Tanks

In retrospect, many people and organizations—including political leaders, think tanks, university faculty, business executives, and journalists—contributed to the development and promotion of the four "pillars" of President Reagan's economic program. At each of the various stages of the public policy process a different array of "actors" was on stage.

Several major Washington-based think tanks, as well as many other organizations, played a role in developing national interest and public support for cutting the Federal Budget. Nevertheless, the appointment of David Stockman as budget director surely was a key action on the part of President Reagan. As for the Reagan tax cuts, the general notion came from the President directly. The specific composition of the tax changes drew heavily on the Kemp-Roth legislative proposal and the work of the experts on the Reagan Task Force on Tax Policy.

In the regulatory area, a combination of key Washington-based think tanks and academic economists was responsible for making regulatory reform a national issue as well as developing the underlying justifications. The specific proposals that were adopted arose primarily from the regulatory experts on President-elect Reagan's Task Force on Regulatory Reform.

As for monetary policy, the role of University of Chicago economist Milton Friedman was central, both in terms of generating the underlying analysis as well as convincing Ronald Reagan. A variety of economists developed the monetarist approach and ensured that it would get a continuing hearing on the part of governmental decision makers.

Clearly, no one group or individual—other than perhaps Ronald Reagan himself—was responsible for the totality of the Reagan economic program. One participant surely deserves a substantial share of the credit, George Shultz. He led a strategic group in the Fall of 1980, the Economic Policy Coordinating Committee, which succeeded in pulling together the various advisory reports developed for the incoming president. The Coordinating Committee consisted of the chairs of the Reagan economic task forces as well as such economic and political luminaries as Milton Friedman, Arthur Burns, Paul McCracken, Alan Greenspan, William Simon, and Jack Kemp.

In two full days of meeting in late November 1980, the Shultz committee succeeded in integrating the task force reports and other materials in a comprehensive report to the President-elect. On the third day the entire committee presented each of the proposals to Ronald Reagan who, under Shultz's astute guidance, discussed and reviewed the material in detail. What emerged became in good measure the Reagan economic program, which commonly was called Reaganomics.

In retrospect, sometimes and for some subjects, notably regulation, think tank scholars played important roles. However, in many other cases such as cutting spending, no think tank was really influential. Of course, the role of several Washington-based think tanks in developing public support for the new policies was important. In a variety of meetings and publications, AEI, Cato, and Heritage played key roles.

All in all, it seems clear that think tanks, especially their joint involvement with university faculty, contributed significantly to the development of Reaganomics, but many other organizations and individuals were also involved. To restate the obvious, the role of Ronald Reagan himself was central to the enterprise.

Summary and Integrative Thoughts

Over the years, each of the major DC think tanks has made fundamental (or surely important) contributions to the role of think tanks in public policy.

At the outset, Brookings set the basic tone—a college without students where accomplished scholars devote their efforts to applying their professional tools to key issues of public policy. Brookings' participation in specific issues has ranged from its initial efforts in the early 1920s in connection with the establishment of a budget system for the federal government to its assistance in developing the post-World War II Marshall Plan of foreign aid to its work on campaign finance reform (the latter involved a joint effort of political scientists in Brookings and AEI).

Subsequently, AEI was established to become the loyal opposition in the think tank community. It recruited more conservative researchers to work on problems of public policy, albeit often from a different vantage point than Brookings. As the intellectual center of gravity in the national capital shifted towards the right, AEI became known as more of a mainstream think tank, especially in the area of economic policy. The research it sponsored on taxation and regulation became influential (as shown in the earlier "Case Study" section in this chapter). More recently, the neoconservatives in the defense and foreign policy sections of AEI were a very different breed.

Years later, CSIS joined the ranks of Washington-based think tanks. It focused heavily on military and foreign policy. CSIS tries to bridge the partisan gap by bringing in analysts of different persuasions, often using them as staff to temporary policy committees consisting of business executives, former government officials, and technical experts. Its major accomplishments have related to changes in the structure of military decision making, notably the strengthened role of the Joint Chiefs of Staff.

The creation of Heritage broadened the scope of think tanks in a basic way—by focusing far more directly on the application of policy research to the current issues on which the Congress is working. Although the "war of ideas" widened the partisan divide, Heritage's work forced the other think tanks, notably AEI and Brookings, to adopt a more activist stance. Heritage's role was most visible in the successful effort to move much of the Reagan legislative agenda from proposal to enactment. It also was active in promoting the antiballistic missile system.[34]

Cato, the youngest of the DC-5, has staked out a distinctive libertarian position on public policies. In the process, it has demonstrated that integrity of research is not necessarily limited to academics and their approaches.

The result is a very lively competition of ideas and methodology in the public policy arena—far greater than most critics realize. Perhaps that intellectual sense of competition, rather than any impact on individual policy decisions, is the most fundamental and durable contribution that the major think tanks have made to American public policy over the years.

Notes

1.   Andrew Rich, *Think Tanks, Public Policy, and the Politics of Expertise* (Cambridge: Cambridge University Press, 2004), p. 208.
2.   *Ibid.*, p. 76.
3.   Donald E. Abelson, *A Capitol Idea: Think Tanks and U.S. Foreign Policy* (Montreal: McGill-Queens University Press, 2006), pp. 172-173.
4.   *Ibid.*, p. 177.
5.   Tim Groseclose and Jeffrey Milyo, "A Measure of Media Bias," *Quarterly Journal of Economics*, November 2005, pp. 1191-1237. In terms of frequency with which legislators cited the work of the DC-5, the rankings were Brookings, CSIS, AEI, Heritage, and Cato.
6.   David M. Ricci, *The Transformation of American Politics* (New Haven: Yale University Press, 1993), p. 2.
7.   Christopher DeMuth, "Think-Tank Confidential," *Wall Street Journal*, October 11, 2007, p. A21.
8.   Author's interview with Christopher DeMuth, Washington, DC, January 21, 2007.
9.   Andrew Rich, *Think Tanks, Public Policy, and the Politics of Expertise* (Cambridge: Cambridge University Press, 2004), 199-200.
10.   Isabel Sawhill and Adam Thomas, "A Tax Proposal for Working Families With Children," *Brookings Policy Brief, Welfare Reform and Beyond*, January 2001.
11.   Author's interview with John Hamre, Washington, DC, May 9, 2007.
12.   Donald E. Abelson and Evert A. Lindquist, "Think Tanks in North America," in James G. McGann and R. Kent Weaver, editors, *Think Tanks and Civil Societies* (New Brunswick, NJ: Transaction Publishers, 2000), p. 58.
13.   Author's interview with Tom Mann, Brookings Institution, Washington, DC, July 17, 2007.
14.   Edwin Feulner, "The Heritage Foundation," in James G. McGann and R. Kent Weaver, editors, *Think Tanks and Civil Societies* (New Brunswick, NJ: Transaction Publishers, 2000), p. 77. For a similar conclusion, presented in a scholarly manner, see Donald E. Abelson, *Do Think Tanks Matter?* (Montreal: McGill-Queens University Press, 2002).
15.   Quoted in Donald E. Abelson, *A Capitol Idea: Think Tanks and U.S. Foreign Policy* (Montreal: McGill-Queens University Press, 2006), p. xi.
16.   William J. Lanouette, "The 'Shadow Cabinets'—Changing Themselves As They Try to Change Policy," *National Journal*, February 25, 1978, p. 303.
17.   David M. Ricci, *The Transformation of American Politics* (New Haven: Yale University Press, 1993), p. 2.
18.   See *Economic Strategy for the Reagan Administration*, A Report to the President-Elect Ronald Reagan from his Coordinating Committee on Economic Policy, November 16, 1980.
19.   "America's New Beginning: A Program for Economic Recovery," reprinted in James Tobin and Murray Weidenbaum, editors, *Two Revolutions in Economic Policy* (Cambridge: MIT Press, 1988), pp. 291-317. See also Murray Weidenbaum, *Advising Reagan: Making Economic Policy, 1981-82* (St. Louis: Washington University, Murray Weidenbaum Center on the Economy, Government, and Public Policy), 2005.

20.   John R. Meyer et al, *The Economics of Competition in the Transportation Industries* (Cambridge: Harvard University Press, 1959).

21.   Thomas Gale Moore, *Freight Transportation Regulation* (Washington, DC: American Enterprise Institute, 1972).

22.   George W. Douglas and James C. Miller III, *Economic Regulation of Domestic Air Transport* (Washington, DC: Brookings Institution, 1974).

23.   Sam Peltzman, *Regulation of Pharmaceutical Innovation* (Washington, DC: American Enterprise Institute, 1974); John P. Gould, *The Davis-Bacon Act* (Washington, DC: American Enterprise Institute, 1971); Rita Ricardo Campbell, *Food Safety and Regulation* (Washington, DC: American Enterprise Institute, 1974).

24.   Murray L. Weidenbaum, *Government-Mandated Price Increases* (Washington, DC: American Enterprise Institute, 1975).

25.   *Reforming Government Regulation*, Report of the Task Force on Regulatory Reform, November 1, 1980.

26.   Four major Washington think tanks—AEI, Brookings, Cato, and Heritage—issued numerous reports throughout the decade of the 1970s on shortcomings in individual government spending programs and in the federal budget process generally. In retrospect, no single report stands out, but the cumulative effect on government decision-makers and the general public was substantial, especially gauged by the extensive media coverage.

27.   David A. Stockman, *The Triumph of Politics* (New York: Harper & Row, 1986), p. 71.

28.   Martin Anderson, *Revolution* (New York: Harcourt Brace, 1988); see also Karen K. Skinner, Annelise Anderson, and Martin Anderson, editors, *Reagan, In His Own Hand: The Writings of Ronald Reagan That Reveal His Revolutionary Vision for America* (New York: Free Press, 2001).

29.   Charles L. Heatherly, Jr., editor, *Mandate for Leadership: Policy Management in a Conservative Administration* (Washington, DC: Heritage Foundation, 1981).

30.   Herbert Stein, *Presidential Economics* (Washington, DC: American Enterprise Institute, 1988), Chapter 8.

31.   Author's interview with Carleton Group member Ernest Christian, Washington, DC, June 18, 2007.

32.   For an array of professional analyses of the Reagan tax cuts and other aspects of Reaganomics, see Federal Reserve Bank of Atlanta, *Supply-Side Economics in the 1980s* (Westport, CT: Quorum Books, 1982); and Laurence Meyer, editor, *The Supply-Side Effects of Economic Policy* (St. Louis: Washington University, Center for the Study of American Business, 1981).

33.   Milton Friedman and Anna Jacobson Schwartz, *A Monetary History of the United States, 1867-1960*, NBER Studies in Business Cycles #12 (Princeton: Princeton University Press, 1963).

34.   Author's interview with Edwin Feulner, president of Heritage Foundation, Washington, DC, October 25, 2007.

8

Findings, Conclusions, and Recommendations

The preceding chapters have tried to make a convincing case for the important role of the major Washington think tanks in influencing public policy in the United States. This final chapter is devoted primarily to offering suggestions and recommendations for dealing with their shortcomings and thus enhancing the contributions that these key organizations make. As I will show, that requires rethinking both their basic missions and the ways in which they carry them out.

I start with five findings and then turn to an array of conclusions and recommendations.

Some Findings on Think Tanks

On the basis of the research performed for this study, I offer the following findings:

1. *Think tank staffers in the aggregate are activists AND scholars.*

Although earlier studies label some of the major think tanks as "activist" and others as centers of research, it is inaccurate simply to put any of these large and complex organizations in one category or the other. Each of them contains individual staff members that could be labeled "activists" or "scholars." However, most of their researchers and analysts possess some of both attributes, although to differing degrees. The scholarly bent is necessary in order to perform creditable research that will have some influence, while a degree of activism is needed in order to insert the work into the public policy process.[1] As AEI President Christopher DeMuth described the situation, think tanks operate "at the crossroads of politics and academics."[2]

Contrary to a widespread belief in academic circles, scholars at AEI, Brookings, and CSIS do not confine their activities to books, journal articles, and other formal publications of their public policy research. They frequently meet with government decision-makers, both formally and informally, in order to promote their ideas. Brookings' Global Economy and Development Program does not sound like an ivory tower operation when it states that "we develop practical ideas for capitalizing on the opportunities presented by globalization…"[3] Similarly, the typical policy analysis by a Cato or Heritage researcher is a well-written and seriously researched piece of work—even if it is not designed to qualify for publication in a learned journal.

Yet, all of these think tank people are of a different breed than the multitude of lobbyists who attempt to influence public policy in behalf of specific clients. Whether benign or misguided, the typical think tank researcher is motivated by ideas, rather than the desires of interest groups.

An important distinction should be made, however, between any of the DC-5 (AEI, Brookings, Cato, CSIS, and Heritage) and some of the newer breed of smaller and more activist public policy institutes, which have been established at the state level. In Kentucky, the Bluegrass Institute for Public Policy Solutions states its purpose quite bluntly, "To force legislators and policy makers to confront bad policy and gaps in performance."[4]

In Arizona, the Goldwater Institute's Scharf-Norton Center for Constitutional Litigation has filed lawsuits in behalf of five charter schools. As a more general proposition, the head of that Litigation Center writes that "litigation (or the implicit threat) can add clout to policy recommendations. A good idea can become a compelling one if lawmakers know that policy recommendations may be followed by a lawsuit."[5] That surely is at the activist end of the policy spectrum!

2. *None of the major think tanks is totally conservative or totally liberal.*

AEI has some former Democratic advisers and Brookings has attracted several well-known Republicans. CSIS has appointed cabinet-level alumni of both parties. Although clearly right of center, Heritage and Cato are hardly substitutable for each other. They differ sharply on defense and social policies—Heritage research tends to be mainstream "conservative" on defense and social issues while Cato's libertarian orientation results in more "liberal" positions. These serious analysts of public policy truly cannot be readily "pigeon-holed" despite their overall philosophies or political orientation.

To some extent, the public policy community comprising Washington, DC-based think tanks has come to a full cycle. Led initially by a basically conservative AEI, an effort was made to offset the liberal dominance in public policy thinking epitomized earlier by the Brookings Institution. With the subsequent rise of the Heritage Foundation and the Cato Institute, it often has seemed that the center of gravity among these public policy organizations had swung clearly to the right.

In recent years, however, several new liberal or Democratic-oriented think tanks have been established. One with particularly strong support from labor unions, the Economic Policy Institute, was established in 1986. Its board of directors includes major labor leaders, notably the heads of the Machinists Union, the Auto Workers Union, and the Service Employees Union.

In 2003, former Clinton White House chief of staff John Podesta founded the Center for American Progress (CAP). With a roster that includes other alumni of the Clinton Administration, CAP operates as part think tank and part self-styled "war room" to respond to issues of the day. Its communications department has a staff of about eighty. A third and even newer democratically-oriented group is Third Way, which targets the Senate Democrats as its prime audience. Six senators serve as co-chairmen or vice-chairmen of the group.[6]

3. *The differentiation of think tanks from universities is substantial.*

To cite the obvious, universities are geared to the education of students while think tanks focus on influencing public policy. At a more general level of abstraction, universities and think tanks share a common fundamental objective. The eminent philosopher Alfred North Whitehead wrote, "The task of a university is the creation of the future."[7] In that spirit, think tanks and universities may represent a division of labor in a grand effort to achieve a common objective.

Think tanks often marshal substantial amounts of resources on a given issue very quickly. This contrasts sharply with the frequent faculty response, "That is an interesting question. I'll try to work on it during my next sabbatical." On the other hand, no think tank has produced the equivalent of Chicago's Milton Friedman or Harvard's Paul Samuelson or Stanford's Kenneth Arrow—people who make a fundamental contribution to their field of knowledge. Of course, that is not the intention of think tank managements (not many universities produce an Arrow, a Friedman, or a Samuelson).

As for the supposedly narrow range of thinking and philosophy in the DC-5 ("they are all so pro-capitalist"), think tanks often contain a broader diversity of viewpoints than I have seen in many university departments. However, *The Economist* goes too far when it states,

"For all their talk of 'diversity' American universities are allergic to the diversity of ideas."[8]

In both the university world and the think tank community, recognized experts—professors at universities and scholars at think tanks—expect to be given a substantial amount of independence in their research as well as in their public activities and statements. When these senior people take controversial stands on public policy issues, they are generally recognized as speaking as individuals and not as representatives of their organizations.

Just as the quality of work and range of interests vary widely among think tanks, so does a similar variety exist in colleges and universities. As someone who has had the opportunity to live in both worlds, I find that a bit of humility in attitudes across the think tank-university divide is surely in order. Moreover, that dividing line is much more porous than popularly conceived.

Most obviously, the typical think tank staffer has been trained at a college or university. Frequently he or she has taught at one or more of them prior to entering the think tank world, or even while in it. Also, quite a few college faculty seek summer or sabbatical-year appointments at a think tank or financing for a study or a job for some of their students. On occasion scholars leave their think tank to take on or return to a full-time faculty position at a university.

4. *Competition among think tanks is pervasive.*

There is intensive competition in the marketplace for ideas and think tanks are major competitors in that market. They constantly vie for visibility and thus for funds, staff, and influence. Each think tank serves as a partial check on the others. Reputation is key to influence in Washington. Shortcomings in a think tank's activities are quickly noted by competing organizations, especially in the informal relationships they have with media and governmental representatives. As a result, competition among the major think tanks is "fierce but civil." Those are the terms of a DC-5 CEO who believes that their relatively sophisticated level of debate on policy ideas contrasts very favorably with the far more partisan posturing characteristic of election campaigns.[9]

The think tank "marketplace" is very open and fluid. There is a continuous ebb and flow of ideas, people, organizations, and influence in the Washington policy community. People move from a think tank to a government position and return to the think tank world, although not necessarily to the think tank with which they were previously affiliated. Also, researchers and analysts on occasion move from one think tank to another, particularly as one organization obtains a larger measure of resources or starts a new and interesting research program. Think tanks are anything but static in their operations, effectiveness, and market position.

5. *Think tanks make a special contribution to public policy.*

Members of Congress, journalists, and others involved in the public policy process are well served when think tanks provide a policy forum for knowledgeable and experienced people. The result is that those participants are not merely reciting standard conceptual theorems, but demonstrate that they have studied the specific questions at issue and often had participated in decision making on public policy in those fields.

We can recall that AEI's William Baroody, Sr. justified the establishment of an alternative to Brookings by repeatedly stating that competition of ideas is fundamental to a free society. In that spirit, political scientist David Ricci offers an even more generous evaluation: "...the sum total of think-tank ideas that circulate in Washington make a commendable contribution to society's perennial search for political wisdom."[10]

Some Conclusions and Recommendations

Because of the importance of their activities—and their tax-exempt status—think tanks should be held to a high standard.

1. *When critics say that think tanks are more tank than think, they are making a serious point.*

Think tanks love to boast of the frequency with which their staff members appear on national television and are quoted in major newspapers. The nation deserves better than the status quo in think tank operations. Providing a free research service to the Washington press corps (and getting yourself and your think tank "mentioned" in repayment) is useful. However, those "plugs" are surely not the key reason for spending over $400 million of tax-exempt dollars a year on these private institutions.

The fundamental justification for the generous support of think tanks is that they are expected to come up with constructive new policy ideas and to actively participate in the lengthy process that extends from presentation of ideas to their incorporation in public policy. There are numerous opportunities for the leading think tanks to do so and a host of unmet needs along these lines.

In practice, seriously influencing public policy is far more than a matter of visibility. Analysts at a think tank do not—or surely should not—view their role as engaging in a combat sport. The development of ideas is a different and difficult activity—and ultimately more satisfying.

The public policy process draws on ideas old and new and reconciles different approaches, viewpoints, and interests. That is a key reason why a comprehensive tax bill, or a clean air act, is so complicated. Rarely if ever does a "clean" bill (one devoid of compromise and complexity) on any major issue attract majority support in the legislative process.

2. *It would be heartening if the major think tanks were less predictable in the positions that their senior scholars take on public issues.*

In the area of economics, it would be striking if Brookings economists came up with economic forecasts and proposals that supported a Republican administration while AEI economists took the opposite position (and vice versa for a Democratic administration). Of course, we would expect strong intellectual consistency in the research and writings in each of these organizations, but something considerably short of the readily predictable.

Many thoughtful citizens are offended, and for valid reasons, by the notion of a "war of ideas." Some think tanks, on both the right and the left, take the position of "us" against "them." I have devoted a substantial portion of my professional career to developing strong and controversial positions that have generated a goodly amount of brickbats. In the process, I have learned that the public policy process is properly viewed as involving a substantial amount of "give and take," and mutual learning.

The possibility does and should exist that your opponent in a particular policy debate is making a valid point that you have ignored. With serious effort and an open-minded attitude, some common ground often can be achieved. That point should not be pushed too far. Some tough policy questions do not lend themselves to easy resolution or "splitting the difference."

Certainly, the new breed of assertive state public policy institutes that are directly involved in litigation truly stretch the traditional notion of what a think tank should do. Suing people and organizations in order to advance specific public policy positions surely strikes me as a stretch too far for a public policy research institute. Edward Crane, CEO of the Cato Institute, comes down even harder on think tanks that "are taking openly partisan political stances that undermine their credibility and threaten the tax-exempt status of...policy research groups over the long-term."[11]

3. *Think tanks are better at analyzing the shortcomings of other elements of society than of their own operations.*

Formally, each of the major think tanks is interdisciplinary, in that it houses researchers with many different backgrounds and capabilities. But the autonomous silos that are found in business and other organizations (where there is little interaction across the various divisions) are just as prevalent in the larger think tanks.

Economists working on domestic issues and political scientists examining questions of foreign policy usually are assigned to different divisions of the organization. Likewise, the Asian experts are rarely contaminated by interaction with the European specialists—or vice versa. Such isolation minimizes the possibilities for real intellectual interaction. To some extent, this specialization of function reflects the organization of the federal government—separate and often competing Departments of Agriculture, Commerce, Defense, State, etc. But that is not a good reason for think tanks maintaining such internal isolation.

Yes, similar criticisms are leveled at universities. However, there is some justification for focusing on training students in the concepts and methods of a single discipline—after they have been exposed to a comprehensive liberal arts and science curriculum. However, the essence of a think tank is to work on public policy. Any practitioner with substantial experience in governmental decision-making knows that there are no purely economic issues or political issues or social issues or security issues. Effective policymaking typically draws on people with a variety of professional backgrounds and policy experiences. As a practical matter, it is far easier for a private sector organization like each of the DC-5 to respond to this basic aspect of policymaking than the far older and more entrenched bureaucracies of the federal government.

CSIS provides a cogent, but hardly unique, example of how a large think tank can pull together expertise from different divisions of the organization to focus on a single issue of public policy. A recent project focusing on the role of China in attracting energy sources in the Middle East drew on analysts specializing in energy, the Middle East, and China. Each staff member was located in a different part of the organization. I mention this example because such intellectual cross-fertilization does not occur very often in the think tank community in general or at CSIS in particular.

4. *The subject of quality control deserves much more attention than it has attained in the think tank world.*

This is a difficult subject to deal with. Researchers are a notoriously independent bunch and do not like their work to be closely monitored or even supervised. I quickly admit to that shortcoming myself.

Yet when approached with care and flexibility, useful efforts can be made to improve the quality of the work done in think tanks and thus enhance their effectiveness. Some think tanks, notably Brookings, have a long-established review process that includes bringing in outside experts to comment on ongoing research or a proposed report. AEI attempts to include in its reviews specialists with very different policy orientations from the authors. Flexibility surely is key. On an urgent matter of public policy, a formal and therefore lengthy review process can mean that the report will not be published until after the issue is resolved.

A suggestion comes to mind based on a popular academic model. It does not involve compromising the intellectual independence of the researcher, but it provides the benefit of advice from others. Many university departments establish a series of seminars at which scholars try out their new research on their peers. The seminar does not attempt to judge the work under review. Rather, those attending merely ask questions and offer comments. The researcher is free to accept or reject the advice. Although the entire process is voluntary, it does serve to enhance the quality of the resultant output. With suitable modifications, this seminar approach should be followed more widely than it now is in the think tank community.

Perhaps the most effective response to the matter of quality control is to present the issue to the staff members of each think tank to face and to resolve on their own. After all, the scholars and researchers in the Washington think tanks have a personal stake in the credibility of the organizations with which they are identified—both in the public policy arena and in their professional fields.

Each of the major think tanks—as well as the entire array of public policy research institutes—can benefit from more directed training of young people in policy analysis and applied research. Exchanges of university faculty and graduate students would enrich both institutions.[12] A two-way movement is needed, including think tank senior staff members taking leaves of absence to serve as visiting faculty at universities as well as more academics spending sabbaticals at think tanks.[13]

A Look to the Future

Looking ahead, it seems clear that the general notion of a wide array of public policy research institutes ("think tanks") active in the nation's capital will continue to be a durable phenomenon of the American public policy scene for the foreseeable future. It is more than a matter of sheer momentum. The different motivations of the numerous financial supporters of think tanks virtually assure the continuation of a variety of these intellectual contributors to the public policy process.

However, it is not written in the stars that the five organizations analyzed here will remain in their present roles or at their current absolute or even relative size. Tough competition will continue to exist for available funding and invariably for attention and influence in the public arena. Specifically, the Aspen Institute possesses the resources—both in terms of a large endowment (over $100 million) and in the current inflow of new revenue (over $50 million)—to attempt to make it part of a DC-6. But that is only a conjecture about the organization's future potential.

Future changes in the mix of public policy issues could well generate comparable changes in the number and nature of these non-governmental institutions that participate in the public policy process by providing the important inputs of information, analysis, and ideas. Some long-time Washington, DC observers welcome the possibility of newcomers to the think tank scene. They see the new arrivals as a counterweight to "old-line" think tanks that become too concerned with maintaining their ongoing relationships with congressional and executive branch power centers.[14]

Changes in the roles and relative importance of think tanks—both those based in Washington, DC and elsewhere—are likely to occur in the future as the result of two very different trends.

The first trend emphasizes greater specialization of labor among think tanks. The success of the major think tanks continues to generate interest in, and financial support for, creating new public policy research institutions. The newcomers—such as the Progressive Policy Institute and the Center for American Progress—are more specialized, either by subject matter or ideological orientation. Like new companies in the business sector, turnover may be especially high at the outset. On the positive side, however, new small enterprises tend to generate a disproportionately large share of innovations.

The second trend operates in the reverse direction. Although public policy debates in recent years have become more vitriolic than in the past, there has been a countertendency on the part of several of the largest think tanks to join forces on key issues. In doing so, they develop common ground in contentious areas or at least set limits to the decibel level of the national debate. The Washington-based think tanks are in a special position to do more of that.

No one knows how these two offsetting forces—greater ideological orientation versus seeking some common ground—will affect the overall role of think tanks in the United States. However, even with little knowledge of future specifics, we can conclude that think tanks will continue to be important participants in the formation of public policy.

This study ends with a very specific proposal. It is based on my varied experiences with five of the key Washington-based think tanks as well as on my reflections as a long-time university faculty member.

Searching for Common Ground

The United States is entering a period of extraordinary policy challenges, domestic and international. One historian sees a near future where the "volatile brew of deficits and demographics...begins to reach a boil."[15] The presence of those policy challenges is becoming widely accepted, although solutions seem to be beyond the immediate horizon. This situation presents an ideal opportunity for the Washington-based think tanks to plow some new ground.

To respond to that combination of challenge and opportunity, another change in emphasis on the part of the major think tanks is in order. The earlier shift to a more conservative and harder hitting "war of ideas" has served its purposes and run its course. It should be soft-pedaled or retired. In the words of Edwin Feulner, the president of the Heritage Foundation, "Our free, self-governing society requires an open exchange of ideas, which in turn requires a certain level of civility rooted in mutual respect for each other's opinions and viewpoints."[16] The shift needed now surely is not to more eloquent justifications for reversing course and returning to a liberal, welfare state.[17]

Think tanks should provide an antidote to the oversimplified sloganeering, liberal and conservative, that dominates political and public policy debates. To use the language of those debates, the nation has gone from a political environment where the prevailing attitude in the economic sphere can accurately be described as, "they never saw a government spending program they did not like" to "they never encountered a tax cut that they did not fall in love with." Neither of these two "knee-jerk" attitudes contributes to a more enlightened public policy or public policy arena.

We can only hope that the policy pendulum does not swing back to the earlier extreme, whether in economics or other public policy areas. Some proposed reductions in taxes merit our opposition, notably closely targeted tax cuts that benefit narrow constituencies. Surely, a similar negative conclusion can be arrived at in the case of very selective increases in government programs and expenditures, epitomized by congressional "earmarks." In earlier days such special interest spending was described more accurately as "the pork barrel."

Properly considered, basic issues of public policy are not matters of either/or but of more or less. Thus, as a nation we care deeply about the environment, but that is not our only or overriding concern. The same point can be made for other key policy issues—whether they be international competitiveness, unemployment, income inequality, or entitlement reform. President Dwight D. Eisenhower made this point very clearly: "It is in the combination of…various attitudes that we hammer out acceptable policies; enthusiasts for anything go too far."[18]

In this spirit, serious changes in public policy call for thoughtful analysis and not bumper sticker sloganeering. It is ironic to recall that, at a time when the educational levels were so much lower than the present, the public arguments over the nation's policies produced such masterly contributions as the essays of James Madison and Alexander Hamilton in the form of the *Federalist* and, somewhat later, the enlightening and extended Lincoln-Douglas debates. The power of modern science and technology enables the society to produce more than thirty-second sound bites for the evening news and "juicy quotes" for the front pages of our newspapers.

The present situation presents an unparalleled opportunity for the nation's think tanks, especially those that are active in the decision-making center of the federal government. These important and strategically located organizations should take on the difficult task of raising the level—and improving the quality—of the national debate. The five major DC-headquartered think tanks should give a high priority to jointly developing more effective ways of dealing with society's problems, domestic and international. Like university scholars, each of them would benefit by submitting their ideas to the informal give-and-take with the counterparts in their sister think tanks.

Funds for such an innovative approach are not likely to come from the traditional sources that think tanks rely upon. A relatively new player, such as the Gates Foundation, may be the most appropriate vehicle. Enhanced leadership at the Carnegie, Ford, and Rockefeller Foundations could also provide the necessary financial incentives for such a radical departure in Washington think tank activity.[19] As a practical matter, the possibility of additional and generous financing for the novel undertaking described here would energize think tank managements to see the benefits of a joint effort to take the high road.

The true mission of a mainstream Washington think tank is not to dominate the print media or the nightly news. Nor is the key function even to influence governmental decision making on a specific law, regulation, or judicial decision. Rather, if there is a fundamental justification for devoting a significant portion of the society's resources to think tanks it is to elevate the level of the national discussion on the serious issues facing the society.

Surely, the public welfare is not advanced by an endless series of sharp and partisan thrusts that ignore the full range of relevant facts and analyses. Like universities, think tanks at their core are educational institutions promoting open-minded thinking and generating new ideas. We will be able to tell that progress along these lines is occurring when a think tank issuing a narrow partisan report is ignored or, better yet, hooted down.

As occasionally they already do, AEI, Brookings, Cato, CSIS, and Heritage should devote more of their efforts to using their particular capabilities to jointly generating innovative policies, which can attract widespread, bi-partisan support. The late Herbert Stein pointed out that second-best answers on which we agree may be more valuable than first-best answers on which agreement cannot be reached.[20]

There is considerable precedence for cooperative undertakings. At the staff level, many of the analysts at these five organizations participate in the meetings and occasionally the research of the others. In several recent cases, analysts of two think tanks co-authored public policy volumes. Increasingly, the organizations themselves are reaching beyond their customary domains to co-sponsor policy events with their traditional competitors and with other organizations, including university-based centers and institutes.

These joint efforts should avoid settling for the lowest common denominator in presenting the results of their combined activities. Candid and balanced appraisals of the pros and cons of specific public policy proposals would help elevate the level of the continuing national debate.[21] At times, the interaction on the part of knowledgeable professionals—whether they come from the right, left or center—can result in surfacing new approaches, which arise above the partisan divide.

Two related long-term developments—the progress in communications technology and the continued impacts of globalization—make the search for common ground by U.S. think tanks more feasible than in the past. The enhanced ability to communicate globally at modest cost permits national institutions to respond more promptly and fully to challenges from other parts of the world. The accelerated integration of the world economy increases the urgency of that response.

Given the high levels of professionalism in many of the think tanks, a fundamental change in the attitude of their managements is vitally important. The compelling need is less for the wielder of the sharpest policy thrust but rather for the lucid synthesizer of the most relevant research and analysis. Likewise, society needs the sensitivity to the long-term concerns of the citizenry more urgently than a rapid response to the opportunities of the moment. Future competition, particularly among the major think tanks, could well be centered, not on achieving greater visibility, but on developing responses to economic, environmental, and national security problems that are more likely to be adopted and carried out.

Think tanks that proclaim their dedication to the pursuit of truth and the principles of freedom would benefit from rereading the message of the distinguished jurist Learned Hand: "The spirit of liberty is the spirit which is not too sure that it is right. The spirit of liberty seeks to understand the mind of other men and women. The spirit of liberty weighs their interests alongside its own without bias."[22]

Notes

1. Richard Haass, president of the Council on Foreign Relations, sounded this theme in a recent Council publication. "It is not enough to produce good work; it must also be disseminated." Richard N. Haass, "The David Rockefeller Studies Program—A World Class Think Tank," *The Chronicle*, April 2007, p. 3.
2. Christopher DeMuth, "Think-Tank Confidential," *Wall Street Journal*, October 11, 2007, p. A21.
3. Brookings Institution, *Global Economy and Development*, July 2, 2007, p. 1.
4. "Kentucky," *SPN News*, July/August 2007, p. 14.
5. Clint Bolick, "A Perfect Match: Litigation and Public Policy," *SPN News*, July/August 2007, p. 1. See also Clint Bolick, *The First Line of Defense: A Blueprint for State Constitutional Litigation to Expand Freedom* (Phoenix: Goldwater Institute, (undated)).
6. Jim Snyder, "Center-Left Think Tanks Gain Ground," *The Hill*, March 29, 2007, p. 1.
7. Alfred North Whitehead, "The Aim of Philosophy," in Daniel Bronstein et al, *Basic Problems of Philosophy* (New York: Prentice-Hall, 1947), p. 705.
8. "Capital of Culture," *The Economist*, October 6, 2007, p. 34.
9. Author's interview with Cato president Ed Crane, Washington, DC, June 19, 2007.
10. David M. Ricci, *The Transformation of American Politics: The New Washington and the Rise of Think Tanks* (New Haven: Yale University Press, 1993), p. viii.
11. Edward H. Crane, "Think Tanks Should Think, Not Lobby," *SPN News*, August/September 2006, p. 1. See also Jonathan Chait, *The Big Con: The True Story of How Washington Got Hoodwinked and Hijacked by Crackpot Economics* (Boston: Houghton Mifflin, 2007), p. 249.
12. Alice Rivlin, "Policy Analysis at the Brookings Institution," in Carol H. Weiss, *Organizations for Policy Analysis: Helping Government Think* (Newbury Park, CA: Sage Publications, 1992), p. 27.

13.   J. David Richardson, "Wanted: More Effective Public Communication in Empirical International Economics," in Michael Mussa, editor, *C Fred Bergsten and the World Economy* (Washington, DC: Peterson Institute for International Economics, 2006), p. 357.

14.   Author's interview with Ernest Christian, tax attorney and former Tax Legislative Counsel of the U.S. Treasury Department, Washington, DC, June 18, 2007.

15.   Kathleen McCarthy, "Anonymous donor: A New Era of Wealthy Foundations Demands a New Era of Transparency," *Democracy Journal*, Spring 2007, p. 107.

16.   Edwin J. Feulner, *Lay Your Hammer Down*, Commencement Address to the 2004 Hillsdale College Graduating Class, Hillsdale, Michigan, May 8, 2004, p. 8.

17.   See Silla Brush, "Back From the Political Wilderness, Left-Leaning Thinkers Are Having Their Day," *US News & World Report*, April 1, 2007.

18.   Cited in Todd Gitlin, *The Bulldozer and the Big Tent* (Hoboken, NJ: John Wiley & Sons, 2007), p. 281.

19.   I am indebted for this approach to Kent Hughes of the Woodrow Wilson International Center for Scholars.

20.   Herbert Stein, *Presidential Economics* (Washington, DC: American Enterprise Institute, 1988), p. 326.

21.   A good example is the CSIS 2006 report, *Judging the Iranian Threat: 20 Questions We Need to Answer*. Equal space is given to two very different responses to each question.

22.   Learned Hand, "The Spirit of Liberty," An Address to the I Am an American Day Ceremony, New York City, May 21, 1944.

Index

Abelson, Donald, 57
American Enterprise Institute (AEI),
    overview, 24
    projects, 25
    role, 23-26
    studies, 94

Brookings Institution,
    finance, 68
    overview, 21
    projects, 22-23, 25
    publications, 25
    role, 20-21
Brzezinski, Zbigniew, 28
Bush, George W., 25, 92
Business Roundtable, 68-69

Cato Institute,
    publications, 33
    role, 31-34
    Web site, 33
Center for Strategic and International Studies (CSIS),
    and the U.S. government, 69
    notable members, 28
    overview, 26
    publications, 26, 28-29
    projects, 26, 28
    role, 26
Congressional Record, 90
Council of Foreign Relations, 75-76

DC-5, *See also* American Enterprise Institute (AEI), Brookings Institution, Center for Strategic and International Studies (CSIS), Cato Institute, Heritage Foundation,
    and the business world, 69, 77-78
    and the U.S. government, 70-74, 90-91
    comparison, 37-44

financial trends, 37-39
list of their major programs, 89-91
overview, 19-35
DeMuth, Christopher, 25-26, 91

Feulner, Edwin, (Heritage), 92
Fiscal Wakeup Tour, 23
Frank, Barney, 81
Friedman, Milton, 97-98
fundraising, 77, 81-83

government regulation, 94-95
government spending, 95-96

Hamilton Project, 22-23
Hamre, John (CSIS), 58, 92
Heritage Foundation,
    overview, 30
    rise, 60
    role, 29-31

IRS Form 990, 9, 15

Krieble, Robert, 69

Laffer, Arthur, 96-97
lobbying efforts, 75-77

MacLaury, Bruce, 83

Organization for Economic Cooperation and Development (OECD), 3
outsourcing, 50-51

Pew Charitable Trusts, 41-42
public policy
    process,
        catalysts, 5
        development, 4-5
        implementation, 6-7
        legislations, 5

research and analysis, 49-51

Reagan, Ronald, 93-94, 96-97
"Reaganomics," 94-96, 98-99
Research networks, 50
Resources for the Future (RFF), 44-45
revolving door phenomenon, 60-62
Ricci, David, 91

Smith, James Allen, 28
State Policy Network, 44
Stockman, David, 95

Talbott, Strobe (Brookings Institution),
    22
tax cuts, 96-97
Think tanks,
    academic view, 67, 91-92, 105-106
    activities, 59-60
    advocacy, 55
    and the business world, 68-69, 75,
        77-81
    approaches, 55-56
    board of directors, 83-85
    business impact, 78
    CEOs, 15-17, 22, 25-26, 57, 92
    competition, 106
    critics, 38-39

defining, 2-3, 7, 57-58, 103
dissemination of results, 51-54, 96
European, 44
expenditures, 10-15
financial contributors, 67-68
financial support, 11-12, 39-40
functions, 49-54
government grants, 15, 79, 82-83
groups, 45-46, 104-105
impacts, 87-101
joint activities, 25, 41-42, 52
limitations, 62-65
lobbying efforts, 15
media coverage, 90-91
publications, 52
reactions toward, 3-4, 56, 104
recruiting, 62
revolving door phenomenon, 60-62
trade policies, 87

Urban Institute, 12

Volcker, Paul, 97-98

"War of Ideas," 29, 100, 108, 112
World Resources Institute, 12
World Wide Web, 33